The Lover at the Wall
3 Plays on Bahá'í Subjects

The Lover at the Wall
3 Plays on Bahá'í Subjects

A New Dress for Mona • Band of Gold

On the Rooftop with Bill Sears

Mark Perry

DRAMA CIRCLE
Chapel Hill, North Carolina

Drama Circle
P.O. Box 3844
Chapel Hill, NC 27515 USA

Email: info@dramacircle.org
Website: www.dramacircle.org

The plays contained in this volume are available for your group to produce. Visit the Drama Circle website for information on royalties and to apply for permission. No performance may be given without written permission.

The Lover at the Wall: 3 Plays on Bahá'í Subjects
  Copyright © 2011 by Mark E. Perry
  ISBN: 978-0-9834701-0-6
  Library of Congress Control Number: 2011925425

       A New Dress for Mona
          Copyright © 2002, 2009 by Mark E. Perry

       Band of Gold
          Copyright © 2010 by Mark E. Perry

       On the Rooftop with Bill Sears
          Copyright © 2004 by Mark E. Perry

All rights reserved. No part of this work may be reproduced or transmitted in any form or by any means, electronic or mechanical, including photocopying and recording, or by any information storage or retrieval system, except as may be expressly permitted by the 1976 Copyright Act or in writing by the publisher, or for limited use in the classroom.

11 12 13 14 15 16   10 9 8 7 6 5 4 3 2 1

'Then he came to a garden wall, and with untold pain he scaled it, for it proved very high; and forgetting his life, he threw himself down to the garden. And there he beheld his beloved with a lamp in her hand, searching for a ring she had lost.'

Bahá'u'lláh, *The Seven Valleys*

Table of Contents

Acknowledgments ix

Introduction xi

A New Dress for Mona 1

Band of Gold 83

On the Rooftop with Bill Sears 195

Glossary 239

Persian Pronunciation Guide. 242

Bibliography 243

Acknowledgments

"A New Dress for Mona" is a major revision of the earlier play, "A Dress for Mona," which was published in 2002 by 5th Epoch Press. A multitude of people assisted in the development of that earlier work, many of whom were credited in that edition. Continued thanks go to Barry and Carol-lee Lane for their support of the piece including the production of a DVD of a 2003 performance. Also, mention must be made of Olya Roohizadegan's book *Olya's Story*, which was a primary source in the conception of the play. For this recent edition, I relied heavily on the unpublished account written by Mona's mother, Mrs. Farkhundih Mahmudnizhad, and translated by Gloria Shahzadeh. This account was first shared with me by Alexei Berteig, who helped craft a series of questions to Mrs. Mahmudnizhad in preparation for the proposed Jack Lenz film, "Mona's Dream." I must also thank Jack Lenz and David Hoffman, who encouraged me to explore the play cinematically, and Dara Marks, whose analysis of my writing was penetrating. My gratitude to Monir R. for her critical insights. Some readers I'd like to acknowledge: Martha, Maaman, Rahil, Kendall, Cindy and Ladan. Thanks also go to Mikko Kuitunen and Naantali Theatre (Finland) and also Hannah Mangenda and the University of KwaZulu-Natal cast for their helpful feedback. Acknowledgment must also go to those who have labored in translating the play: Migdalia Diez (Spanish), Mikko Kuitunen (Finnish) and Peter Hoerster (German). My gratitude goes out to McKay Coble, the UNC Department of Dramatic Art, and the director and cast of the 2010 UNC production: to Joseph Megel for his care and devotion to new work, to the cast that found the meaning of love in Mona's story, and to Lillian for her wholehearted embrace of Mona in the last days of her earthly life.

The play "Band of Gold" has long been in development. Its first incarnation was read in 1998 at the Playwrights Workshop at the University of Iowa, and the early responses of my colleagues and faculty there were important. Several years later, I picked up the idea again, and by 2004, a draft was circulating among some friends. In 2006, we had a small reading, and in 2008, a larger one, and the current draft was finished in 2010. In particular, I'd like to acknowledge the feedback and support of Phyllis Ring, Amrollah Hemmat, Bill George,

Ken Cabot, Luis Dechtiar, Tim Marr, Suzan Kalantar, and Dr. Ataollah Nadimi.

'On the Rooftop with Bill Sears' is mainly an adaptation of the book, *God Loves Laughter* by Mr. William Sears. Special arrangements have been made for this adaptation with the publisher, George Ronald. A couple of other books by Mr. Sears were referred to, including *Thief in the Night* and *All Flags Flying*. My abiding gratitude goes to the late Marguerite Sears, who took time to provide feedback on the play and to share stories of her beloved husband. Many of these stories are included in her book about Mr. Sears, *Bill* (2003). Shirley Macias and the other friends at Desert Rose Bahá'í Institute must also be recognized, along with the friends at Green Acre Bahá'í School who attended the play's first reading. My gratitude also goes to the donors and crew of the 2004 production, and to my dear colleagues, J. Chachula, Mike Brooks and Bill George.

I am grateful to Tim Marr, Ashley Lucas, Erica Toussaint and Barry Lane for their helpful feedback regarding the introduction and general preparation of this compilation.

Finally, I'd like to acknowledge with loving gratitude my wife, Azadeh, who is the first to read and give feedback on whatever I write. She it is who has helped me raise up these children of the mind and heart. I'd also like to acknowledge my parents for their support and encouragement over the years. Given their role in raising me up, only God can reckon how they have contributed to these plays.

Introduction

From the fall of 1982 to mid-June 1983, Mona Mahmudnizhad—the teenaged protagonist of "A New Dress for Mona" and scores of other innocents like her languished behind prison walls in Iran. They hoped and prayed for release, not knowing when it would come or what demands would come with it. Throughout that time, Mona and those others clung to one thing, and this is why their story is told and retold. They clung to love—a seemingly superhuman love, and they held on to the very last. At the time, I hadn't heard of Mona, though I had learned, even living on the other side of the globe, something of the persecution of her community. Still, it didn't rank so high on my list of personal concerns. During that same period, I was in a prison of my own. It was called the seventh grade.

Social isolation. Rigid protocols and hierarchies. Assaults on individuality. Group showers. If seventh grade wasn't prison, it was good training for it. I was in a new, larger school, and friends were few. I tried sports with unimpressive, even embarrassing, results. I did fine academically, I liked most of my teachers and the principal, but seventh grade wasn't about academics or teachers or administration. It was about other seventh graders, and especially those special few—the cool crowd—who acted as the guards at the gates, deciding who was in and who was out, making and breaking the rules as they would, because they could, because they were cool, and cool is the supreme virtue in a landscape dominated by anxiety. There they were, eating their hot lunch of pizza and chocolate milk, entirely neglecting the vegetable offering, living large, lording it over the bustling cafetorium, while I skulked about, looking for a corner seat to unwrap the bag lunch lovingly made by my mother and consisting of peanut butter and honey on whole wheat. If only I could disappear, but no. My family was struggling financially, and I had to wear those shiny discount knockoffs and not the Timberland boots everyone else was wearing. What ecstatic heights of ridicule those kids on the bus attained as a result! Then my stepfather started to substitute teach at my school to make the extra $27 a day. To get to the school though, he would ride the bus with me. This was not a city bus, mind you, but a yellow school bus. He was gracious enough to sit in the front seat while I hung my head, scuffed my boots and did the dead man's walk to the back.

Day after day, I would come home and plop down in front of my Atari 2600 or else set out on lonely walks through the woods and down the railroad tracks with my dog, Lady Di. I did not have what it took—the character training, the support network, whatever—to adequately withstand this daily barrage. My religious upbringing to this point was an untended garden. Or rather it was an untended plot in a large, fallow field. I was a New Englander, and we were a people with ancient roots in religious values, but nowadays we were Christian largely by circumstance, and "do unto others" was less influential than the default philosophy of "do whatever the h#!! thou willest." I had a spiritual impulse, but some of the religious messages that were coming through were hindering me. They seemed to be either fear-mongering ("The devil is going to get you!"), or judgment-laden ("Everyone else is going to hell") or morally-unsettling ("Do whatever you want; you just have to ask for forgiveness after"). These extremes did not mix well with the intuitive sense I had, even as a pre-adolescent, of the divine purpose. The secular world, on the other hand, seemed to offer just surface sincerity or cynical alienation. Most people seemed to cope with this world through materialistic pursuits, obsessive competitiveness, and all manner of intoxicants. That seemed to be the path that was laid out before me too if I didn't find a creative outlet or a cause to work for greater than the pursuit of my own pleasure. From the deepest heart of me, the cry must have gone up: God, get me out of this mess!

Then, an epiphany. It was during a school performance of "My Fair Lady." I was not on stage, but in the audience. While the play that night may have proved a slight test of endurance for supportive parents, it catapulted me into another realm. What was this event that could so transform this space? To me, it seemed as if the roof had been blown out, and the rules that governed our world were suspended. We were freed, transported to some liminal space between this junior high cafetorium and Edwardian London's Covent Garden. Here an eighth grade geek could channel a passionate, witty Englishman. Kids who, in the hallway that very afternoon, would sooner drink toilet cleaner than take a false step were now singing, dancing, wearing makeup, and braving cockney accents, risking public exposure on a whole new scale. Here there was support though, even for the missteps. False notes still won applause. Here was a process that affirmed both individual expression and creative collaboration. Here our minds and feelings as audience merged and swayed this way and that not according to some immediate private concerns but following some urgent shared priority—fictional, yes! And on the surface, it had nothing to do with our lives, but it spoke to something deeper, to a common condition of being human across space and time. I enjoyed the play that night, but it was the phenomenon of theatre that bowled me over. The next year I would try out for the school play and—lo!—would be cast in a lead role. I had found a creative outlet, or it had found me, but either way life would never be confined again.

Another life-changer was in the works as well: less immediate, but more revolutionary. My stepfather—whom I liked—had moved into our home that summer, and along with various exotic items from his world travels came all these books about this religion with a funny, foreign name. My suspicions were on high alert for anything cult-like, or anything non-Christian for that matter. Further investigation though would gradually reveal not only that this religion posed no threat, but that it gave answers that resolved in simple terms the several paradoxes that had confounded my awakening religious sensibility. I found it offered a clear, embracing vision of our world and our existence, and it allowed a place for me in the divine plan. It affirmed the oneness of God and spoke of the world's religions not as competing armies on an apocalyptic battlefield, but as successive chapters in one ongoing, divinely-guided educational process carrying humanity ever forward. Its central principle was unity among the world's peoples, and it sought the elimination of prejudices and other barriers to that unity. It was at once idealistic and pragmatic, easy to understand while retaining a mystical orientation. The problem I found, however, was its name. The unfamiliar name "Bahá'í" along with the name of its Founder, Bahá'u'lláh, seemed to keep people from looking at what this Faith had to offer. These names stood like a hefty wall blocking the way of a generation that could only gain by considering the beautiful, synthesizing teachings inside.

It came to me only gradually what now seems obvious, that I should combine these two gifts I'd received. The Bahá'í writings spoke highly of the station of drama. They raised engagement in the arts to the level of worship and claimed art to be "*a gift of the Holy Spirit.*" The task though was a bit daunting. There was no established network to plug into, no touring circuit to join. The Bahá'í Faith is still young to have birthed a substantial artistic culture and still too far out of the mainstream consciousness to have gained a voice in the general theatre community. I did encounter others along the way who shared the vision of Bahá'í-inspired drama, and their work and their encouragement emboldened me. Over time, the calling became clear. I would strive to use this profound expressive outlet of drama to explore Bahá'í stories and themes and communicate these universal teachings to a general audience. People wouldn't need to subscribe to a new religion to benefit from spending an hour or two meeting characters who strive for spiritual transcendence and social transformation, or absorbing themes of racial harmony, religious tolerance and multicultural exchange. An audience would happily suspend its disbelief for a story that dug deep into the human soul and emerged with hope in hand. So what of one proclaiming that, despite the present darkness, a glorious future awaits humanity as we mature and move out of this traumatic period of our collective adolescence? Adolescence, after all, may feel like it's going to last forever when you're in the midst of it, but reason and experience say otherwise.

The Lover at the Wall

Here then are three plays inspired by the history and teachings of the Bahá'í Faith, but intended for a wider audience. They have been long in coming, two of them having taken over a decade to find their current form. They are also, each one of them, deeply personal. I have laughed and cried my way through them, wrangled my brain, that you might do the same.

"A New Dress for Mona" is a play about the young Iranian martyr, Mona Mahmúdnizhád. Mona was a beautiful 16-year-old, full of life and promise, when, in 1983, she was executed, alongside nine other Bahá'í women, for no crime greater than teaching a children's class. Her remarkable faith and her supreme love were encapsulated in her final earthly act, when she kissed the hand of her executioner and the noose placed around her neck. To achieve such a station, however, Mona first had to triumph over fear and move past the natural anger towards injustice, and that journey is the focus of the play. "Band of Gold" is an ensemble piece set in suburban Florida about the surprising impact an engagement announcement has on the families of the interracial and cross-cultural young couple. Just because Chris and Tahirih are both Bahá'ís does not mean they are guaranteed an easy path to marital bliss. Here is a play that examines with humor and pathos the complex undertaking of integration and of building unity at its most fundamental levels, that of marriage and family. "On the Rooftop with Bill Sears" is a one-man show based on the life of Mr. William Sears (1911-1992), a figure much loved in the Bahá'í world and one who offered much love and joy in return. Having achieved some celebrity in early television, he struggled to harmonize his career ambitions with the higher calling of service. Set in a TV station in Philadelphia in 1953, this play dramatizes a critical moment in Mr. Sears' life and testifies to the truth reiterated by Bahá'u'lláh that "*one hour's reflection is preferable to seventy years of pious worship.*"

Love is at the heart of these plays, and the characters here are each, in some sense, suffused in love. There's the conventional pairing of young lovers eager to wed in "Band of Gold," who stand amid married couples that may once have been love-blind youth, but now face the challenges brought by love at their relationships' current stages. There's the distant admiration of the young guard for Mona, and then there is Mona's awakening to a profound, consuming love to burn away all earthly appearances. With "On the Rooftop," there is the child's pure search for unconditional acceptance in place of parental indifference, a search that will only yield its full results years later, in love's perfectly inconvenient manner.

Here are lovers on their respective paths—some well-ahead and sprinting, some caught at a fork in the road, some dallying, and indeed some moving backwards. Each, in their way, offers an example to ponder. The phenomenon of drama permits us, as audience members, a kind of objectivity when we look at their situations that we often lack when looking at our own lives. Here we may sit and watch, defenses down, in a capacity similar to that of the seeker spoken of by Bahá'u'lláh in his great mystical work, *The Seven Valleys*:

> "*In this journey the seeker reacheth a stage wherein he seeth all created things wandering distracted in search of the Friend. How many a Jacob will he see, hunting after his Joseph; he will behold many a lover, hasting to seek the Beloved, he will witness a world of desiring ones searching after the One Desired.*"

The supreme example of love in Persian lore is Majnún, the insane one, who sifts through the dust in search of Laylí. Bahá'u'lláh recounts this ancient tale in *The Seven Valleys*, where we find Majnún steeped in the pain of long separation from his love, such that he cannot eat, he cannot sleep. Friends avoid him, and family cannot talk sense into him. He has let go of sense, for "*when the fire of love is ablaze, it burneth to ashes the harvest of reason.*" Majnún longs for death just to stop the pain. And so he sets out one night into the streets determined to end his life, and yet when confronted by the city's watchmen, he runs, fearful of the same. He runs and runs until he is cornered. And so, Majnún "*came to a garden wall, and with untold pain he scaled it, for it proved very high; and forgetting his life, he threw himself down to the garden. And there he beheld his beloved with a lamp in her hand, searching for a ring she had lost.*"

It seems it is not enough for the lover to tread the path of love, nor is it sufficient to sigh and pine. The lover must go to the wall. That is, the character of one's love must be proven, tested as gold in the fire, made evident in a climactic display. Majnun faced adversity and seeming injustice, personified by the watchmen, but he persevered and pushed on. He forgot himself and found his beloved. And as with Majnún, so too with the characters in these plays: that which he feared, that which he ran from, turned out to be the means of his delivery.

In sharing this story, Bahá'u'lláh adopts and deepens the Sufi casting of the Majnún and Laylí story in a spiritual light, where Majnún is symbolic of the sincere, seeking soul and Laylí is the emblem of the Divine Beauty. Here then is an object-lesson not of the tragic turns of earthly love, but of that soul pure enough to attain the Divine Presence. This lover is an athlete in the spiritual arena, and the victory is the triumph over self. The opponents are the allied ranks of misbelief, of doubt, of apathy, of passivity, of distraction, of envy, of malice, of ambitiousness, and of fear. In this light, Majnun's lengthy period of separation tested the quality of his devotion. Such a one as holds any contradictory impulses is not yet ready, and if the so-called lover quickly moves on in pursuit of another, the superficiality of the love is revealed, torn up like a shallow-rooted weed. If, however, the lover is true, then such roots will only deepen with time, reaching out in all directions in search of the loved one. Love is, after all, manifest not only in lack of concentration and an inability to sleep. As is said in *The Hidden Words*, "*The sign of love is fortitude under My decree and patience under My trials.*" And when the time of real trial arrives, when the lover comes to the wall—partly impelled by internal need, partly compelled by outward circumstances, then that lover will need to dig down deep to muster the strength and the volition to mount that final obstacle, and then that soul may find itself, by the aid of the All-Merciful, delivered from the barren valley of remoteness to the blissful garden of reunion.

Here drama would appear the very able chronicler of the soul's test, for it cuts to the quick to find individuals in crisis, the lover at the wall. A recurring theme in so many stories is that the protagonists are called—as if from the plane of the spirit—to purify their moral characters, to so narrow and intensify their desires that only one choice remains, where there is no longer a dilemma, no longer a conflict for there is no way to return to the old ways once the crisis reaches its apex. Once at the wall, Majnun could only think to go up.

Not all characters will rise to the heights to which they are summoned, neither will all souls. Mona did, after her father did, after so many other martyrs. Mr. Sears did, though he might be the first to say his sacrifice was less absolute. The fictional characters in "Band of Gold"—well, they're all over the map, like most of us who are currently sheltered from the storms afflicting so much of humankind. We may think that, by avoiding war, famine, revolution and other external crises, we are free from being tested. But those who would count themselves among the lovers of God must, according to Bahá'u'lláh, awake and *"bestir ourselves"* to hear the cries of our fellow creatures and answer the urgent needs of our day.

There is a new standard of love in this Day. As part of humanity's awakening maturity, we are being called to a higher spiritual station, both individually and collectively. We are entering a period in which, Bahá'u'lláh says, the *"assayers of mankind"* will *"accept naught but purest virtue"* and when *"deeds done in the gloom of night"* will *"be laid bare and manifest before the peoples of the world."* In this day, for example, steadfastness in one's faith is no longer the standard, but rather that joyous acceptance displayed in the face of grievous persecution by such heroes as Mona. There's also a new standard of love in family, in marriage and in community. Models of inter-cultural unity barely conceived much less achieved in past ages are now coming into being, as portrayed in "Band of Gold," as the diverse peoples of the planet accelerate their joyous, painful and irreversible convergence into a single human family. Beyond these examples still, a new standard is required in our professions and everyday lives. People of goodwill, people who share the Bahá'í vision of individuals rising in service to reshape human civilization, the same must consider how they might venture out of the comfort of their everyday social roles, as Mr. Sears did, and commit themselves, sacrificially even, to realizing that vision.

In the life cycle of humanity, this is a new age, an age of astonishing capacity, in which we are reaching for our social and spiritual maturation, the glorious birthright of our kind. We stand now collectively before a wall, the staggering height of which will require, if we will top it, everything we've got. This is the hardest climb we'll ever know, and yet what a garden of delight waits on the other side: the Kingdom on earth as it is in heaven, the realization of our essential unity.

A NEW DRESS FOR MONA

A two-act play based on the life of
Mona Mahmúdnizhád (1966-1983)

To the Bahá'ís of Iran

Setting

Shiraz, Iran. 1982-83
(A few years into the Islamic Revolution)

Cast of Characters

Mona (Mahmúdni<u>zh</u>ád)	16; bright, passionate, single-minded, not yet a saint.
Father (Yadu'lláh Mahmúdni<u>zh</u>ád)	50; gentle, loving, with a youthful exuberance and a compelling manner.
Mother (Fár<u>kh</u>undih Mahmúdni<u>zh</u>ád)	Late 40s; anxious, strong-willed, tender-hearted.
Árám	20ish. Quiet, with a poetic streak.
* Mulla	A powerful religious cleric, adamant.
* Farah	16; bold and worldly, Mona's friend.
* Mrs. <u>Kh</u>udáyár	Middle-aged; loyal, a close neighbor.
* Taráneh (Mahmúdni<u>zh</u>ád)	23; kind, pragmatic, Mona's sister.
* Guards 1 & 2	Members of the Revolutionary Guard.
* Woman in White	A messenger from the World of Light.
* Teacher (Female)	Narrow-minded, but not without pity.
* Rezá	20ish; a homebody, Mrs. Khudayar's son.
* Shopkeeper (Male)	An opportunist who thinks he's principled.
* (Mr.) Ehsán (Mehdizadeh)	31. Bahá'í martyr and apparition.

These roles may be assigned from among an ENSEMBLE of 6-8 actors. each of whom plays multiple characters. Other speaking and non-speaking roles include Mr. Vahdat, Mr. Khushkhú, students (female), worshipers, spirits, people on the street, vendors, young children, prisoners (female), guards, and baby Núrá.

Historical Note: Characters other than Mona's family and the Bahá'í martyrs are fictional, often being composites of the actual figures involved in the events portrayed.

A NEW DRESS FOR MONA

ACT I, Scene 1 – Mona's home

A soft light illumines MONA, *alone.*

MONA: Iran, Iran—Once the pearl of the world, exalted among nations. You lit the Sacred Fire. You rebuilt the Holy Temple. Placed gifts before a newborn King. You took on the Prophet's mantle and embraced His family. Iran, my Iran—what has happened to you now? You raise up your enemies and mow down your friends. You lock up wisdom and lift the foolish. You reward thieves and sacrifice your heros. How far you have fallen, Iran... and how ever will you rise again?

A night bird is heard. Lights come up. We see a large rug, a window frame, a tape recorder on a table, some candles and matches, plus a large poster board, paint, photos, scissors, and other crafts. MONA *is now on the rug and plays a recording of herself chanting. She lights three candles as she speaks the following names.*

MONA: Ehsán Mehdízádeh. Sattár Khushkhú. Yadu'lláh Vahdat.

As she lights each candle, three blindfolded men are illuminated upstage one by one.

MONA: Friends, what can I offer up for you? I'd say my life, but I don't think God is interested in that. So I will paint you a picture.

She starts to paint. An execution scene starts to play out around her. The three men are in light, but the GUARDS *are not. They wear masks covering their mouths and noses.*

GUARD 1: Traitors! Heretics! You are to be executed now because of your crimes against Faith and Country. What do you have to say?

MR. KHUSHKHU: O God! Take me!

MR. VAHDAT: Guard! Come.

GUARD 1 motions a younger guard, ARAM, towards MR. VAHDAT.

GUARD 1: Go.

He goes.

MR. VAHDAT: You think I'm a traitor? My name is Vahdat. I was a colonel in the army.

GUARD 2: You were a colonel, then you became a... what was it?

GUARD 1: (*Taunting.*) Auxiliary Board Member!

GUARD 2: And for that you die! Plus the rest of you!

MR. KHUSHKHU: O God!

MR. VAHDAT: Take off my blindfold. I'll watch the bullets come.

ARAM looks back to GUARD 1, who gestures him on. He removes the blindfold.

MR. VAHDAT: (*Softly.*) Just don't aim for my heart. That does not belong to you.

MR. KHUSHKHU: O God!

GUARD 2: Be quiet!

EHSAN: Guard! Take mine off too. I will also welcome the bullets.

ARAM, with clearance, goes to EHSAN and loosens his blindfold. The GUARDS are edgy, as if they're being mocked.

GUARD 1: Okay!

ARAM turns to go.

EHSAN: Wait. Give me your hand.

EHSAN kisses ARAM's hand. MONA's vision of the execution seems to pause and we see this detail disturbs her.

ARAM & MONA: Why did you do that?

The execution resumes.

GUARD 2: No use begging for mercy! It's time to die!

GUARD 1: (*To a bewildered ARAM.*) Get back here, stupid!

ACT 1, SCENE 1

ARAM *returns.*

GUARD 1: Ready!

MR. KHUSHKHU: We thought the days of the martyrs had ended.

GUARD 1: Aim!

GUARD 2: Aim for the heart!

The GUARDS *rain bullets on the men.* ARAM *is unable to raise his gun. Mona's* MOTHER *has entered.*

MOTHER: Mona?

MONA *has dipped a paintbrush into red paint and now brushes it liberally on the picture she is making.*

MOTHER: My God, girl, what are you doing?

MONA: Remembering the martyrs.

MOTHER: We don't know that it's true, Mona. That woman who brought the news, she's a very emotional type. They'll run you up and down the wall if you let them. Watch the rug. Look, your father has gone to find out what really happened. So until he comes, just put it outside your mind.

MONA *dips her hand in the red paint and begins to smear it over her picture.*

MOTHER: Now you're just trying to provoke me. Let's get your clothes ready for tomorrow. You haven't worn this green dress in a while, does it even fit now you're filling out?

No response.

MOTHER: What color are you going to wear?

MONA: Black.

MOTHER: (*Takes a deep breath.*) Don't you have homework?

MONA: I have an essay on how Islam brings freedom into our lives.

MOTHER: And?

MONA *looks at her as if the answer is self-evident.*

MOTHER: So talk to them about true Islam, not the regime, but the teachings of Muhammad: pray to God, give to the poor...

MONA: Why do you think Ehsan kissed the guard's hand?

MOTHER: We don't know that's true.

MONA: Who would make up such an odd detail?

MOTHER: Someone who wants attention! When people want attention, they embellish stories... (*Seeing the photos.*) You cut up all our pictures? Okay that's it. (*Blows out the candles.*) You need to just stop this and go to bed.

MONA: Mom, our friends have given their lives. What small sacrifice can we make?

She lights a match to relight the candles. The FATHER *is at the door.*

FATHER: Alláh-u-abhá. [1]

MONA: Dad. (*Blows out her match.*)

MOTHER: Tell us something good.

FATHER: (*After a beat.*) They're free.

MOTHER: What? What do you mean they're free? Free-free?

MONA: They're gone, Mom.

MOTHER: What? (*To* FATHER.) Then why didn't you say that? O God! I don't believe they killed them. (*Goes to leave.*) I don't know why you said that, Jamshid.

She is gone. MONA *has lain down on the carpet. The* FATHER *comes to her. They are quiet a while. He wipes her hand, caresses her hair.*

MONA: You're next, aren't you?

FATHER: We don't know that.

MONA: After Mr. Vahdat, you're next in line.

FATHER: Maybe things will calm down.

She hears the gunfire.

MONA: (*Without emotion, at first.*) So we're just supposed to lie down and let them roll right over us, mow us down one by one because we're a peaceful people they can scapegoat, we don't just not put up a fight, we welcome death, we welcome the bullets, we kiss their hands...

---

[1] A Bahá'í greeting meaning 'God is most glorious.'

FATHER: Don't go too far now.

MONA: I'm not kissing anyone's hand.

She kisses his. He strokes her hair.

FATHER: Don't talk about this with your mother, okay?

MOTHER: (*Entering.*) What?

FATHER: (*Smiles gently.*) We have a funeral to arrange.

ACT I, Scene 2 – Mona's School

A school for girls. A STUDENT *fervidly reads aloud her essay.* MONA *is drawing a picture. Nearby is her friend,* FARAH.

STUDENT: Heaven opens its gates and calls out "Enter me!" Blood gathers on the ground and calls out "Avenge me!" The Revolution gathers momentum and calls out "Serve me!" Islam is the tree planted by Heaven watered by the blood of Revolution and its fruit calls out "Eat me!"

Some students giggle at this, including FARAH. *She turns to* MONA, *who is intent on her drawing.*

FARAH: (*Quietly.*) You're not drawing flowers today.

MONA *shakes her head.*

FARAH: Is that you?

MONA *nods her head.*

FARAH: You have fire in your eyes.

MONA: So watch out.

FARAH: What's going on?

MONA: (*Changing subject.*) Do you have your essay?

FARAH: Yeah. My brother wrote it.

MONA: I thought you were going to write this one yourself.

FARAH: I tried—swear to God, but the topic is so boring, so unrelated to my life. Just get me through this school year, and I'll live a hundred percent honest life. (*She smiles.*)

TEACHER: (*Unseen.*) Farah, would you like to read your essay?

FARAH *stands to read.*

ACT 1, SCENE 2

FARAH: " 'The fruit of Islam is liberty and freedom of conscience, but you must taste it to understand.' Our great leader, Ayatu'llah Khomeini, has brought us back from the dangerous path of westernization the Shah was pursuing. We are returned now to the path of Muhammad, the Imams, and the law of the Qur'an. The West teaches that sweetness is found in boundless freedom, in material possessions, in satisfying the appetite, in alcohol, drugs, sex... (*She grimaces.*) Here they offer us a fruit that looks sweet, but tastes bitter, as they spread around the world this lie they call liberty when they only seek to enslave other nations in order to gain more themselves. But here is true sweetness, like a bite of ripe pomegranate: to submit to God's decree. May the righteous live forever with seventy-two virgins... And may the infidels burn until they turn black as coal." (*A beat.*) Sorry I got a little carried away at the end there.

TEACHER: Mona?

MONA *stands. She is timid at first, but soon grows impassioned.*

MONA: "Freedom. Of all the great words in this great wide world, freedom is the greatest. Throughout history, people have craved liberty. They've written about it, sung about it, fought for it, died for it. And yet, some men...

In the background, we see the silhouette of a religious cleric, MULLA, *ascending a pulpit.*

MONA: (*Cont'd.*) ... out of some perverse element of their soul that craves power and control, have insisted on denying liberty to others. They became like animals, like wolves in their pursuit, hunting down helpless gazelles, and they kill them, and roll in their blood, and their eyes roll back in their heads and so are blind to the evil they perpetrate...

TEACHER: I think that's enough.

MONA: (*Facing off.*) Why do you deny liberty to Bahá'ís?

Silence.

TEACHER: Sit down, Mona.

MONA: We are your countrymen, the same blood. Don't we have the right to live and believe what we will?

TEACHER: Stop right there.

MONA: What are you afraid of? That we'll steal away your freedom?

TEACHER: Students, turn your backs and put your fingers in your ears.

MONA: Or that we'll steal this veil you're hiding behind?!

TEACHER: Farah, you too! Right this minute.

The TEACHER *is now there, just outside of the lighted area.* FARAH *reluctantly turns her back on* MONA.

MONA: (*With fire in her eyes.*) Throw down that veil!

She throws down her paper. The STUDENT *who first read her essay traps it beneath her foot. Jump to next scene.*

ACT I, Scene 3 – A Mosque

The Islamic call to prayer is heard. The Shí'ih Muslim cleric, MULLA, *from the previous scene speaks, addressing a congregation.*

MULLA: The Revolution is triumphant! The light of Islam is spreading throughout the land! Praise be to God! He has sent our supreme leader, Ayatu'llah Khomeini, and has cast down the tyrant Shah. Many years we waited, many years while corruption festered, while he suppressed us and squandered the wealth of our nation on his passions and western friends. How does it feel now, Muhammad Reza? Now you are king over a few cubic meters of foreign dirt? (*Pause.*) Let us talk about a quiet corruption, let us talk about Bahá'í. Now Bahá'ís don't fight, and they don't force. They smile, and they help, and they trickle in like oil into your well water, like a potion in your tea. This corruption must be eradicated from this land. Where is the faithful believer who will assist me? For this is not only a revolution, but the Judgment, when the righteous and the sinners must be separated, and when those in the middle—who fail to take a side—will be hacked in two by the sword of God.

The crowd chants "Alláh-u-akbar" (God is great!) with exuberance. The MULLA *comes and joins* GUARD 1, *who attends as if protecting the* MULLA *as he walks through a crowd. The* MULLA *points out a woman.*

MULLA: See how beautiful this woman is? See how her beauty acts on you? How it starts bringing up your desire, driving your thoughts toward sexuality? This is the power of the devil. Not to say she's the devil, exactly, but her allure the devil uses to lead us astray. This is why we make hijab universally applicable. Now it's true most women don't get the fire going, but here in Shiraz, there are enough girls, a man can't walk in the street without seeing them with the short skirts and T-shirts. It's a good thing I have a robe like this, but a plain-clothes brother on the street...

GUARD 1: I think she wants to speak to you.

MULLA: (*Gestures him away.*) Flee the devil.

The GUARD *exits. The* MULLA *is approached by a* WOMAN *and her daughter (the* STUDENT *from the school scene). Both are shrouded in dark chadors and their voices cannot be heard.*

MULLA: Sister, I'm very happy you've come. This is your daughter, she must resemble more your husband. Of course, you can kiss my hand, but it's the Imam in me that accepts, otherwise those lips...

She kisses his hand.

MULLA: ... could give a horn to a holy man.

The daughter (STUDENT) *hands him Mona's paper.*

MULLA: What is this? (*Looks and listens.*) And the name of this Bahá'í girl? Hmm. I'll certainly look into that. You know, daughter, you should work in the company of men, your appearance is highly conducive to an atmosphere of chastity.

Another kiss for the hand.

MULLA: Another kiss then? Oh, and the daughter. Well, okay.

The two are gone. GUARD 1 *returns with* ARAM, *the reluctant guard from Scene 1.*

MULLA: These Shirazi women!

GUARD 1: Your eminence, you remember my cousin, Aram?

MULLA: He looks like he needs some sleep. What's going on with these Bahá'ís? What happened at the cemetery today?

GUARD 1: (*Caught off guard.*) Nothing, things were fine, we were in control. (*A beat.*) People get emotional sometimes.

MULLA: (*Unsatisfied, to* ARAM.) Were you there?

ARAM: Yes, sir.

EHSAN, *the martyr from Scene 1, has entered, now as an apparition. He stares at* ARAM.

ACT 1, SCENE 3

MULLA: And?

ARAM: I was just trying to keep calm.

MULLA: So they were making trouble?

GUARD 1: We had it under control.

MULLA: Not you. (*To* ARAM.) They were angry?

ARAM: They were mourning. Some were angry.

MULLA: The Bahá'ís?

> EHSAN *has opened his coat to reveal blood.*

ARAM: I couldn't tell Bahá'ís from Muslims.

MULLA: You can always tell. (*Points to his own eyes.*) Would you like me to teach you how?

ARAM: I like to learn.

MULLA: Oh, he's slippery. That wasn't what I asked you.

GUARD 1: He's a poet-type, sir.

MULLA: A poet? So, Hafez, let's hear one.

ARAM: My memory's not so good.

MULLA: So compose one. I'll give you a subject: the Bahá'ís. Who was it you were following?

> EHSAN *has come close to* ARAM.

ARAM: Ehsan.

MULLA: Last name, I mean.

ARAM: Mehdizadeh.

MULLA: Good memory. So describe him—no poem necessary, just a word.

> EHSAN *takes* ARAM'*s hand to kiss.*

GUARD 1: Say something, Aram. He was a spy, a traitor.

MULLA: (*To* GUARD 1.) Shut up. (*To* ARAM.) Hafez?

ARAM: (*After a pause.*) Mystifying.

GUARD 1: (*Hits* ARAM *on the head.*) Idiot!

MULLA: Shut up! Go bring me my rug. It's time for prayer.

The GUARD *goes to kiss the* MULLA's *hand, but he's waved away.*

MULLA: You live in your thoughts, don't you, young man? Yes, some of the Bahá'ís seem to embody remarkable virtue, whether forgiveness, courage... tolerance for pain. But true virtue is born of submission to God's will, you see?

ARAM *gestures as if he has heard and is considering the matter. He watches* EHSAN *move away.*

MULLA: Okay, Hafez, I'll be looking for a job for you, one we wouldn't want to waste on just any lughead.

GUARD 1 *is back with the prayer rug. The* MULLA *offers his hand in dismissal to* ARAM, *who goes to shake it. The* MULLA *is surprised, but not phased. When* ARAM *goes to pull away his hand, the* MULLA *holds it, twists is just so, looks it over.*

MULLA: Soft. What would people say if they saw that the Revolutionary Guard had such soft hands?

The call to prayer has begun again. The MULLA *goes into his preparations. The* GUARD *gives* ARAM *a look.*

ACT I, Scene 4 – Mona's Home

MONA *and her* MOTHER *enter—the* MOTHER *with a dark chador, which she removes and folds up upon entering.*

MOTHER: Your father already has so much on his mind with the martyrs needing burial and the guards refusing us going in to the cemetery... It's only because he pleaded with that man that you weren't expelled.

MONA: You should have let them do it.

MOTHER: Are you so ungrateful? You're one of the few Bahá'í children still in school.

MONA: What am I learning? Propaganda! It's not like I can go to university anyway.

MOTHER: Look, we are going to get through this. These mullas can't stay in power long. The people will see the violence and they'll say enough is enough.

MONA: We can't just wait to be rescued while they sweep into our homes and take what we love.

MOTHER: They won't. God won't let them.

MONA: God let them into Mr. Vahdat's home. Being a Bahá'í is no protection—that goes for Dad too.

MOTHER: Your father is going to be fine! People were mad they couldn't go pay their respects to the dead. The Muslims, I mean. They will push back...

MONA: In one hundred forty years, when have the people of this country ever stood up for us? (*A beat.*) We have to sound the alarm, remind them that this is Iran, the land of Cyrus the Great, the founder of human rights! That's what I was standing up for today.

MOTHER: Did it work?

MONA: Did what work?

MOTHER: Your wake up call.

MONA: No, because the teacher made them put their fingers in their ears.

MOTHER: And this is what they will continue to do if we speak to them harshly.

MONA: What does God want us to do, Mom? If He just shows me the path, I'll go. I just don't understand why there has to be so much pain. (*Waits for an answer.*)

MOTHER: Why are you looking at me?

A knock. The door opens. It's Mona's sister, TARANEH, *23 and pregnant.*

MOTHER: Taraneh!

TARANEH: Hey, I got here as soon as I could.

MOTHER: You need to talk some sense into this sister of yours.

MONA: Ah, ah, ah, ah, ah....

MONA *goes right for* TARANEH*'s belly. She kneels and touches.*

TARANEH: Hi darling.

MONA: (*Absorbed.*) I can't believe this is you, Taraneh. There's a little creation forming inside of you.

TARANEH: Yeah, I'm inflating like a balloon. God, I hope I can save my skin.

MONA: (*In her own world, but not leaving* TARANEH*'s belly.*) But imagine what the baby is going through, no idea where life is leading. Bahá'u'lláh says we're like the baby in the womb and the spiritual world is all around us. You know, like we're inside, hidden by this veil... (*Indicates her belly.*) All warm, we'd stay inside there forever.

TARANEH: All your meals delivered, I can't believe what food this kid orders, things I never would eat, but she wants it, she gets it.

MOTHER: She?

ACT 1, SCENE 4

TARANEH: Did I say that? I keep telling myself not to. (*Tears well up.*) I don't even want a girl. I think Sírús's family wants a boy—they won't say it, but they keep calling it a "he."

MOTHER: We need a boy in the family.

MONA has her ear up to TARANEH's belly.

TARANEH: What do you think, sweetie?

MONA: I'm listening. (*Addresses the baby.*) Who are you? Helloooo.... Hellooooo.....

A shift where focus comes in on MONA and TARANEH's belly and off the MOTHER and TARANEH's actions. MONA sees a beautiful WOMAN IN WHITE.

MONA: Who are you?

The ceiling seems to open and light starts coming down—a glimmering of the possible.

WOMAN IN WHITE: (*With gentle authority.*) Prepare yourself. Just like the expectant mother, just like the babe—prepare yourself.

MONA: For what?

The WOMAN shrugs as if to say "what else?"

MOTHER: Mona?

Shift back to the physical plane.

TARANEH: Ouch. Honey, you're squeezing a little tight there.

MONA: (*Coming back to herself.*) Huh?

TARANEH: What's wrong? You see a ghost?

MONA: (*Standing.*) No, I'm fine.

MONA exits.

MOTHER: What am I going to do with this girl? She's in her own world half the time, and who can blame her? This one is such a mess, but I'm really starting to worry. What if they come for your father? She's so attached to him. I catch them sometimes just staring at each other as if they're reading each other's minds. I think they don't want me to know how they're feeling, like it will crush me. It won't! (*She sits.*) I don't know that we shouldn't get out of Iran altogether at least until this whole thing blows over.

TARANEH: Have you talked to Dad?

MOTHER: When do I see him? Anyway, he won't talk about it.

TARANEH: Where is he now?

MOTHER: Where is he ever? Out feeding the poor, healing the sick...

TARANEH: Mom.

MOTHER: I'm sorry, but what about us? And now I see Mona going the same way—you know she's going to this orphanage three times a week now, these tiny neglected kids call her "Mommy Mona," and she just melts. Then she comes home, and the smell! I mean, that's fine, it's great, but the girl doesn't communicate with me! We never had that trouble, you and me, did we?

MRS. KHUDAYAR, *a neighbor, enters.*

MRS. KHUDAYAR: Well, are you coming?

TARANEH: Hello, Mrs. Khudayar.

MOTHER: Coming where?

TARANEH: The birthday party, Mom. I'll get Mona. (*Exits.*)

MOTHER: I can't believe I forgot. What time? Wait til you hear...

MRS. KHUDAYAR: He's just about to cut the cake.

The voice of her son, REZA, *is heard from the hall.*

REZA: (*Off.*) Is she coming?

TARANEH: (*Having reentered.*) Maybe a little later.

REZA: (*Poking his head in.*) Why not now?

TARANEH: Happy birthday, Reza.

MOTHER: Mona has some thinking to do.

MRS. KHUDAYAR: Thinking, huh?

REZA: (*Exiting.*) Fine.

MRS. KHUDAYAR: I keep telling him to get it out of his head, but listen to me? God help us, these little boys grow to be men.

TARANEH: Well, shall we get some cake?

MRS. KHUDAYAR: Well, well, Taraneh, look at you. Wait, wait.

She feels her hair, hikes up her skirt to look at her ankles and legs, feels around her stomach and chest, etc. Then when the exam is over.

MRS. KHUDAYAR: Definitely a girl!

They exit. MONA *reenters, checks the door and peeks around where the* WOMAN IN WHITE *appeared. Finding nothing, she makes a decision and starts to set up her art supplies in a way reminiscent of the first scene. She plays her tape recorder, lights a candle and begins to paint.*

ACT I, Scene 5 – Mona's Dream

MONA *is stretched out asleep.* The WOMAN IN WHITE *from the previous scene enters, radiant. A number of figures,* SPIRITS, *enter.* ARAM *is upstage center, a white shroud thrown over him. The* WOMAN IN WHITE *wakes* MONA *and brings her to her feet.*

WOMAN IN WHITE: I have something for you. A gift. But you must choose.

As MONA *orients herself, three* SPIRITS *with gift boxes come forward. The* WOMAN IN WHITE *gestures* MONA *to the first.* MONA *opens the box and pulls out a beautiful red dress.*

MONA: Ooh.

SPIRIT 1: Red. The final testimony, indisputable truth; blood spilled presents its own proof. Red is a fire, a lover, a warning. The sun descending has no finer adorning.

MONA *holds the dress up to herself. There is an instant scene shift to a girl being executed by hanging.* MONA *shudders and pushes the dress away.*

MONA: No!

In an instant, the scene shifts back and that dress is whisked away. The WOMAN IN WHITE *gestures* MONA *towards the second box.* MONA *goes and pulls out a black dress of the same pattern.*

MONA: Lovely.

SPIRIT 1: Black. Wrapping itself about, the jealous lover douses all other color. Pupil of the eye, closed lid of night; black is nothing without light.

She holds this dress up to herself. An instant scene shift where several people are suffering intolerably, from torture or deprivation. MONA *pushes this one away as well.*

MONA: No, I don't want that one either.

ACT 1, SCENE 5

The scene shifts back, but MONA *is hesitant to open the third box. The* WOMAN IN WHITE *smiles and opens it for her. She pulls out a blue dress.*

MONA: I like blue. (*She takes it, but hesitates to put it up to herself.*) But what is it?

SPIRIT 3: Blue is the beginning, sea and sky, renewal. A soul alone, a stone, a pool. Ripples and reflections that sparkle over faces, good deeds that light up darkened places.

Here the WOMAN IN WHITE *comes close and whispers in her ear.* MONA *hears, holds the dress up to herself.*

WOMAN IN WHITE: Do you want to remove the veil?

MONA *looks at her with all sincerity and nods. The* WOMAN IN WHITE *nods as well. All attention shifts to the shrouded* ARAM. MONA *walks up to him and with a breath pulls off the veil. An unworldly power and radiance rolls off him, and* MONA *is awestruck. All others look away out of reverence.* MONA *has dropped to her knees and stares.*

WOMAN IN WHITE: Enough!

The dream is over. Lighting shift. All leave except ARAM *and* MONA, *who tosses in sleep on the rug and cries out as if falling. Her* FATHER *is there at the door.*

FATHER: Honey? (*He goes to her.*) Wake up, sweetheart.

MONA: (*Waking, crying out.*) Ah! Ah! Dad, Dad...

FATHER: It's okay, sweetie. It's just a dream.

MONA: Dad, I saw Him. I saw Him.

FATHER: It's okay...

MONA: I saw His face.

ARAM *has remained in the same place, as if he's still in Mona's sight.*

ACT I, Scene 6 – A Clothing Shop off a busy street

A SHOPKEEPER *fiddles with a tape recorder that plays music by Dariush, a popular Iranian singer. He sings aloud to a sad, albeit Western-influenced song.* MONA *enters energetically, interrupting him.*

MONA: Salaam.

SHOPKEEPER: (*Wary, turning down the music.*) Salaam.

MONA *is on a mission, searching through the clothes.* FARAH *enters.*

FARAH: Mona, why didn't you wait up for me?

SHOPKEEPER: Salaam.

FARAH: Hi. (*To* MONA.) Are you still mad about the class?

No response.

FARAH: I'm sorry, but what was I supposed to do? Everyone was freaking out, looking at me with all this hate, and the teacher singled me out...!

SHOPKEEPER: Girls, we just got in some nice scarves...

MONA: No thank you.

FARAH: Look, if anyone should be mad, it should be me. You're the one who made a scene, and they all know I'm your friend.

MONA *looks at her.*

FARAH: Got you to look.

MONA *looks away.*

FARAH: Come on, don't be mad at me.

MONA: I'm not mad. If no one will stand up for us, even our friends, when things get tough, that's fine.

FARAH: I told you I was sorry.

ACT 1, SCENE 6

MONA: So I forgive you.

FARAH: But you're still mad. You can't forgive someone and still be mad at them.

MONA: I don't want to talk about it. If you want, you can help me look for a dress.

FARAH: Okay. (*A beat.*) How about a red one?

MONA *looks at her, a little spooked.*

FARAH: Red for anger.

SHOPKEEPER: Very good prices on these scarves, the best in the city!

FARAH: No thanks!

MONA: I don't want red. I want blue. I had a dream last night and I was offered a choice of red, black or blue dresses, and so I chose blue.

FARAH: Offered by who?

MONA: By God. I think.

FARAH: Wow. Why do you think God wants you to have a blue dress?

MONA: The dresses symbolized paths I could choose in my life.

FARAH: Okay.

MONA: The red one meant martyrdom and the black one suffering.

FARAH: Someone would choose those paths?

MONA: I chose the last one, which was service.

FARAH: So…

MONA: I chose a life of service.

FARAH: What about a life of fun?

SHOPKEEPER: (*Approaching.*) How can I help you girls?

MONA: Do you have any dresses this color?

SHOPKEEPER: Sure. Over there.

> MONA *moves to the indicated area. The* SHOPKEEPER *sees* ARAM *standing just outside the shop door looking in, and he goes to switch cassette tapes for something more Islamic.*

SHOPKEEPER: How did that tape get in there? That music's unclean! (*Switches tapes to something more Islamic.*) Much better.

ARAM *seems to take no notice, but stares at* MONA. *He wears nothing that might distinguish him as a guard.*

FARAH: So maybe you're going to get married.

MONA: What?

FARAH: How else do women serve in Iran? They keep the rice cooking and the babies coming.

SHOPKEEPER: (*Back to help.*) God willing. How about this one?

MONA: Mmm, that one.

She chooses a blue closer to the dream color and turns to the mirror. FARAH *browses, then approaches her.*

FARAH: So was there a guy in this dream?

MONA, *having seen* ARAM, *stands transfixed, and points to him. He sees her point and looks away.*

FARAH: What, him?

MONA: (*Folding up.*) Maybe we should buy this and go.

ARAM *is still in sight.* MONA *glances at him as she goes to pay.*

MONA: How much?

SHOPKEEPER: For you: 100.

FARAH: Rial?

SHOPKEEPER: (*Sarcastic.*) Rial. 100 Tuman.

MONA: Sorry I don't have that much.

SHOPKEEPER: Why don't you ask your boyfriend? (*Indicates* ARAM.)

MONA: He's not my boyfriend.

FARAH: Who made you a mulla to judge?

SHOPKEEPER: I have a reputation to keep. Girls like you come in with no scarves, flirting with boys, acting like this is the time of the Shah? Now if you covered your hair like chaste Muslim girls…

MONA: (*Calmly.*) Well, I'm not a chaste Muslim, I'm a chaste Bahá'í. And I can offer you 20 tuman.

FARAH: (*Flummoxed.*) You don't need to tell him that.

SHOPKEEPER: Bábí?

MONA: Bahá'í. They stopped calling us Bábís a hundred years ago.

SHOPKEEPER: Bábí báhí, I don't care. (*He takes the dress back.*) 200 tuman! Final price.

MONA: Sir, be fair. All religions teach that much. (*She pulls out money.*) Now how much is the dress worth? I have twenty-five tuman.

A beat. He looks at her money.

SHOPKEEPER: Out.

MONA: What?

SHOPKEEPER: The dress is not for sale, Bábí girl!

MONA: It's Bahá'í. Bahá'í, Bahá'í, Bahá'í, Bahá'í!

FARAH *walks away.*

MONA: What is the big deal that no one can stand to hear that word?

SHOPKEEPER: Get out!

MONA: Fine. See you, Farah.

On her way out, she passes by ARAM. *They have a moment, and she turns and leaves.*

FARAH: Wait up, Mona! (*To* ARAM.) What are you staring at?

She leaves. ARAM *pulls a photograph from a small notebook, looks at it, then towards where* MONA *exited.* EHSAN *is now there, but* ARAM *avoids looking at him.*

SHOPKEEPER: You go now, you'll lose your girlfriends.

EHSAN *is gone.* ARAM *turns and walks into the shop and picks up the cassette tape of Dariush the* SHOPKEEPER *was playing. He shakes it and puts it up to his ear as if to listen to it. He then raises his eyebrows at the* SHOPKEEPER, *who freezes.*

ACT I, Scene 7 – Mona's Home

Mona's FATHER *and* MOTHER *sit quietly in their living room. There is tension in the air, as if he's delivered news she did not want to hear.*

FATHER: Aren't you going to say something?

MOTHER: What do you want me to say? You're not coming to me asking me my opinion on this.

He is silent.

MOTHER: Have you thought about the impact this will have on Mona?

FATHER: Yes.

MOTHER: She needs a father.

FATHER: Farkhundih.

MOTHER: I am not blowing this out of proportion—

MONA *enters through the front door, mumbling under her breath. She slips off her shoes.*

MONA: Alláh-u-abhá. (*She heads towards her room.*)

MOTHER: Mona, come back here, please.

MONA: (*Returning.*) What's going on?

MOTHER: You told me you'd be back before this. This place needs to be cleaned. I'm going shopping. I'm writing a list for you. I want you to get started right away—

MONA: Okay.

MOTHER: I'm not happy about you being gone when there's so much to do. (*She exits to the bedroom.*)

MONA: What happened?

FATHER: It's okay. (*Exits to kitchen.*) You want a little tea?

MONA: (*Sits on the carpet and holds her head.*) I don't know. (*A beat.*) I saw God today... on the street.

FATHER: (*Reentering.*) You did.

The FATHER *has put the kettle on and now somewhat distractedly tries to straighten up the apartment, which in truth is already quite tidy.*

MONA: There's this path opening in front of me, but it's totally dark. I can't seem to open my eyes wide enough to take it in.

MOTHER: (*Entering, moving to the door.*) Here's the list, Mona, so don't forget. (*At the door.*) There's a package here. Maybe it's a bomb.

She kicks it inside the door and leaves. The FATHER *winces some and holds his stomach.*

FATHER: Mmm.

MONA: Your tummy? Here, let me do that (*She takes the broom.*)

FATHER: I'm okay, I'll just get the tea. (*Exits.*)

MONA: (*Starting, then stopping the sweeping.*) Here's what I figure. I'm not supposed to have that dress. It's just a symbol. I mean, obviously, He told me it stands for service. So I don't need the actual dress for that. It's better that I don't have it.

FATHER: (*Off.*) Uh-huh.

MONA: The young man is a symbol too. He's... the "man on the street"—meaning, I'm supposed to serve everyone, no matter where I am. And... I don't have to go looking for it like I did with the dress. Service will find me. What do you think?

FATHER: Sorry, honey, the kettle was making noise.

He has entered with a tray with tea. He has been crying and turns to wipe away tears.

MONA: Are you sure everything's all right?

There's a knock at the door. We hear the neighbor, MRS KHUDAYAR.

MRS. KHUDAYAR: (*Off.*) Hello!

MONA: (*At the door.*) It's our neighbor.

FATHER: (*Uncertain what to do with the tea tray.*) I better not.

He exits back into the kitchen.

MONA: Dad, come back.

FATHER: (*Off.*) Mona, we can't push people.

MONA: (*Shakes her head and opens the door.*) Hello, Mrs. Khudayar.

MRS. KHUDAYAR: Am I interrupting?

MONA: No, Dad was just making some tea.

MRS. KHUDAYAR: (*So the* FATHER *can hear—*) No thank you.

FATHER: (*Off.*) Hello, Mrs. Khudayar.

MRS. KHUDAYAR: So, Mona, your mother was telling me about your dream—three dresses, that's wonderful!

MONA: Well, it wasn't about dresses really...

MRS. KHUDAYAR: Oh?

MONA: It was really about choices in life...

MRS. KHUDAYAR: Mona, if you just say yes to this boy, these dreams won't haunt you any more.

MONA: What?

MRS. KHUDAYAR: Oh, as if...! Oh! (*Aside to* MONA.) Your father doesn't know yet? The boy who's following you. It's been days now I've seen him.

MONA: What does he look like?

MRS. KHUDAYAR: See for yourself. You can probably spot him out that window.

MONA *walks over and looks out the window, sees him and responds by pulling away and then looking again.*

MRS. KHUDAYAR: (*Excited.*) Oh, oh, oh—do you know him?

MONA: (*Almost to herself.*) That's the same young man as was in my dream.

MRS. KHUDAYAR: Oh, that's so precious. Run away with him! I mean, with your parents' permission and all—

MONA: That wasn't really the spirit of the dream. He was just...

MRS. KHUDAYAR: Just what?

MONA: A symbol.

MRS. KHUDAYAR: Symbol! I don't know about you girls today, with so many boys swarming around you, you take it for granted, then you become my age and you're invisible and have to get your pleasure by watching others, but you're giving me absolutely no pleasure!

MONA: Dad, isn't that tea ready yet?

MRS. KHUDAYAR: Girl, how old are you?

MONA: Sixteen.

MRS. KHUDAYAR: When I was sixteen, I was already married with a loaf in the oven. You're not going to get any more beautiful, my dear.

The FATHER *enters with the tea, still fighting off his stomach pain.*

FATHER: Here we are…

MRS. KHUDAYAR: Look at the time, and I just dropped by to give you some mail, which they delivered to the wrong address. There's one for you, Mona. It arrived unsealed—those goons with the Revolutionary Guard can't admit they're censoring the mail so they try to put it off on me.

MONA: (*Taking the envelope.*) Wait, won't you have some tea with us?

MRS. KHUDAYAR: (*Going.*) That son of mine is going to be home any moment. He was so disappointed you missed his party—Such a lovely rug!

MONA: Mrs. Khudayar, why don't you ever have tea with us?

FATHER: Mona, if she needs to go…

MRS. KHUDAYAR: I have tea at home.

MONA: I know, but we always offer and you never accept.

FATHER: Mona dear.

MRS. KHUDAYAR: No, it's okay. The truth is that from the time I was a little girl, I have been told that your tea—Bahá'í tea—is a potion that brainwashes people to become Bahá'ís.

MONA: But that's silly.

MRS. KHUDAYAR: I know, but what can I do? I guess I'm brainwashed myself. (*Leaving.*) Looks like a package here. Maybe it's from an admirer. (*She winks and leaves.*)

MONA: Don't say anything, Dad. We have to confront these people... as a service to them.

FATHER: (*Unconvinced.*) What's the letter?

MONA: It's been opened.

FATHER: Who's it from?

MONA: (*Opens the letter and reads.*) It's from the Bahá'í children's committee.

FATHER: Yeah?

MONA: They want me to teach a Bahá'í children's class.

FATHER: Let me see.

MONA: (*Moved.*) It's happening, Dad. I asked Him to show me the path and He's doing it.

FATHER: (*Taking the letter.*) I'm just surprised the committee didn't hand-deliver it.

MONA: (*Goes for the package by the door.*) Could be from an admirer. Could be a bomb. (*Picks it up.*) Why was Mom so upset? Before I die.

FATHER: I've been appointed to the Auxiliary Board.

MONA: (*After a beat.*) That's such an honor.

FATHER: And she's worried, obviously, about the exposure.

MONA: (*Covering her emotion.*) Just leave me your books—Taraneh wants them too, but I'll use them more.

FATHER: Mona, I know it's scary, but you know this path God is laying out before you? I have mine too. And your mother has hers. And if God decides that our paths should diverge, I need you to be strong. Okay?

He kisses her and turns to go. She opens the package and pulls out the blue dress from the shop.

MONA: Dad.

He turns.

MONA: Farah must have gone back... (*Holds it up to herself.*)

FATHER: It's as if Bahá'u'lláh picked it out Himself.

Shift of scene. MONA comes forward as if to a mirror with the dress.

MONA: It's a new dress for Mona. And a new Mona must step into it.

ACT I, Scene 8 – A Street in Shiraz

People are coming and going: men freely, women less so. Birds and traffic are heard. ARAM *waits, apparently for* MONA. *He is preoccupied, apparently writing a poem in his notebook. He recites some lines aloud to test them out.*

ARAM: In a perfect world... In a perfect world, there would be no... No... (*Searching for the word.*) Division? Distance? No you and me, but only we.
(*Smiles at this, scribbles and continues reading a line he already has.*) But now I follow, I follow, I follow behind.

He then looks up to see EHSAN *before him. He looks away, moved, as if the brief moments of respite only refresh the agony. The* MULLA *enters with* GUARD 2. *The* MULLA *has an unopened pomegranate.*

MULLA: Hafez! I've been wondering about you.

ARAM: Hello, sir.

MULLA: So? (*Hands* GUARD 2 *the pomegranate.*) Open that up.

GUARD 2 *looks at him quizzically. The* MULLA *focuses in on* ARAM, *waits.*

ARAM: (*Shrugs.*) Just a sweet girl.

MULLA: So she isn't speaking out at all about her religion?

ARAM: Really just going to school, visiting the orphanage... She went shopping with a friend.

MULLA: For what?

ARAM: A dress. I think. Maybe a scarf...

MULLA: (*After a beat.*) Okay. (*To* GUARD 2, *who is vigorously going at the pomegranate.*) Easy there. (*He grabs some seeds and puts them in his mouth. To* ARAM.) Let me see her picture again?

ARAM: Oh. (*Takes the picture out of his notebook.*) I'd be happy to keep it, I mean keep an eye on her.

MULLA: (*Looks at the picture, smiles.*) I'm sure you would. (*Takes back the pomegranate from* GUARD 2, *puts more seeds in his mouth. To* ARAM.) Keep a log of everything she does. It'll help us make a case against the father.

He exits with GUARD 2. ARAM *returns to writing in his little notebook, just as* MONA *and* TARANEH *enter.* TARANEH *wears a loose headscarf and waddles as she walks.* MONA, *wearing the blue dress, walks with a spring in her step and carries a bag with materials and snacks for her children's class.*

TARANEH: (*Offhandedly.*) I don't know, you know, she's Mom, and Mom's not Dad. They're not in the same place. None of us are. I don't even know where I am, and carrying this life inside me, literally creating it as we speak, and I don't know the first thing about her, or him... whatever. So you have your lesson for the kids?

MONA: Yes. (*Sees* ARAM *waiting for her.*) Hello.

She and TARANEH *walk past.* TARANEH *adjusts her scarf.*

TARANEH: You know him?

MONA *doesn't answer as they exit.* ARAM *smiles wistfully, finishes a thought he was writing in his little notebook, and then walks off after* MONA.

ACT I, Scene 9 — The Children's Class

MONA *tells a story to a group of children about 6 or 7 years of age. She is animated, gentle and luminous when she is with the children*

MONA: Once upon a time, there was a lover named Majnun and his love was the beautiful princess, Layli. Majnun was a good man, a pure man, and he had no thought but for his Layli. The problem was he had been separated from her for such a long time that he got very, very sad. One night, he was so sad, he went out into the city hoping to die. And he walked and walked the streets, crying, until a watchman saw him. This was one of the guards in the city. So the watchman started to follow him, and Majnun got scared. He thought the watchman was coming to hurt him. So he walked faster. And the watchman walked faster. And Majnun started to run. And the watchman started to run, and then another watchman came after him, and then another. Certainly these men would kill him, he thought. And so Majnun ran and ran until he got trapped with a tall wall in front of him and all the watchmen behind him. So what do you think he did? He ran to the wall, the men came after him, and so he jumped and he climbed, and the wall was very high, and he worked so hard and they could almost reach him, but with his last bit of strength, he threw himself over the wall not knowing what was on the other side. And he fell and he fell and he landed, plop. And it was soft and green. He was in a beautiful garden, and when he looked, who did he see but Layli walking in the garden, a lamp in her hand, searching for a ring she had lost. So what do you think Majnun did? He cried out in joy, and he thanked God and he thanked the watchmen who had led him to his heart's desire, and he understood that these men he thought were mean and bad and scary actually had done him the greatest service. And he wondered, why couldn't I see that before?

ACT 1, SCENE 9

As she has been finishing this story, ARAM *has appeared in the background, looking in, as if through a window, then he walks off.*

MONA: Did you like that story? That's a story Bahá'u'lláh told. Yes, sweetie.

A child has a question.

MONA: Well, it means that God asks us to be patient with the difficult things in our lives, because what we love most God will never ever really take away even though it may feel like it. What do you love most? Your Mommy and Daddy? (*Smitten and moved.*) Me too. So who wants some cheese puffs?

ACT I, Scene 10 – The Street Outside

FARAH *waits outside where* MONA *has been teaching.* MONA *comes in, high as a kite from being around the children.*

MONA: Farah! I didn't expect you here.

FARAH: I was hoping I could catch you.

MONA: Did you see all my kids?? Aren't they adorable? I just love them so much. I tell you, I feel like I'm right there with God when I'm with them, they fill me with so much light.

FARAH: Yeah, they're cute—you're not mad at me.

MONA: How could I be mad?

FARAH: Cause of the shop.

MONA: (*She models her dress.*) Look!

FARAH: Is that the dress?

MONA: What do you think?

FARAH: It looks great. So look, I don't have much time, but I have to say something. I felt awful about turning away from you in the shop after the whole school thing. I mean it's hard being around you sometimes. I mean I love you, but this... religion of yours... It's a tough thing. But I made a decision: no matter what, from now on, I'm going to stick by you, okay?

MONA: (*Wants to believe her.*) Okay.

FARAH: (*Breathes out.*) Good, I think I forgot some of the things I was going to say—so how did you finally get the dress?

MONA: How did you get it is my question? What did you have to pay that guy? I mean, I'll pay you back.

FARAH: I don't know what you mean.

MONA: Don't play. You bought the dress and left it at my door.

ACT 1, SCENE 10

FARAH: I did?

ARAM has entered and stands at a distance. He is drawing in his notebook with considerable care.

MONA: Didn't you?

FARAH: Maybe. Will you be mad if I didn't?

MONA: No.

FARAH: Then I didn't.

MONA: So who did? No one else was there... (*She turns to look at* ARAM.) Oh no.

FARAH: What? Hey isn't that the guy?

MONA: Yes.

FARAH: What, you think he bought you the dress?

MONA: (*Turns away from him and collapses some under the idea.*) Oh now it makes sense.

FARAH: But who is he? Has he talked to you?

MONA: No, he's following me, but he hasn't said anything. Now I'm wearing his gift he probably thinks we're engaged.

FARAH: Are you going to give it back?

MONA: (*Torn.*) I have to.

FARAH: (*Looks over at* ARAM.) He's pretty good looking.

MONA: Farah!

FARAH: What? Your God is the one who set you two up!

MONA: I've got to get this off. Can you go ask him?

FARAH: What?

MONA: If he gave it to me.

FARAH: Uh...

MONA: I have to know.

FARAH: Fine, but I have to go right after.

MONA: Go, go.

FARAH: All right. (*She approaches* ARAM.) Hey, do you know anything about this dress?

ARAM: (*Holds up his hand and walks away.*) Sorry.

FARAH: Hey, come back, I just want... (*Returning to* MONA.) He walked away.

MONA: What kind of lover is that?

FARAH: I've got to go, but I'm serious about what I said, okay?

They kiss each other on the cheek, and FARAH *leaves.* MONA *looks off the way* ARAM *exited. She slips out of sight. A moment later,* ARAM *enters, looking around for her. He writes something in his notebook.* MONA *sneaks up on him and grabs the notebook, startling him.*

MONA: Who are you and why are you following me?

ARAM: Give it back.

MONA *has retreated so that a tree or a bench is between them.* ARAM *tries to walk around, but she evades him.*

MONA: Don't make me look in your book.

ARAM: Don't.

MONA: (*Reads from his book.*) "I follow wherever you go, Til the light is spent. But then who needs eyes? I'll follow your scent."

ARAM: You have no right to read that.

MONA: (*Relieved, still evading.*) So you're a poet. And an artist?

Some photographs and papers have fallen out of the notebook. MONA *bends to pick them up.*

ARAM: Just leave those!

MONA *picks up a photograph and looks. Lights come up on* EHSAN *just as when he was being executed.*

MONA: Why do you have Ehsan's picture? (*Realization. Gunfire.*) You killed him.

ARAM: Give me that back.

MONA *drops the notebook and turns to walk away as if she has encountered a great evil, fighting a nightmare's paralysis.* ARAM *picks up his things.*

ACT I, Scene 11 – Mona's Home

Home now, MONA *has taken off the blue dress as if it was contaminated. She sits on the rug, shivers, wrapped up in a blanket.*

MONA: O God. O God. O God.

Her FATHER *enters.*

FATHER: Mona? Honey, what's going on?

MONA: (*Covering u.p*) I'm fine. (*Heaving in fear or with tears.*) I'm just cold.

FATHER: Hey, what happened? (*No response.*) Come on, talk to me.

MONA: He's a guard.

FATHER: Who?

MONA: (*Nods, and shivers.*) I think he killed Ehsan.

She throws her arms around her FATHER *and starts to sob, really sob.*

FATHER: What is this?

MONA: O God, Daddy, I don't want to lose you.

FATHER: (*Tries to comfort her.*) Come, come. Hey, I'm still here.

MONA: But you don't know! There might be someone following you too.

FATHER: My dear, someone's been following me for years.

MONA: See! Dad, this isn't funny. We should go now, get out of Shiraz, stay with friends until this passes.

FATHER: (*Listening attentively.*) We could.

MONA: Yes, we could.

He looks at her lovingly.

MONA: So?

FATHER: So who would take care of those who can't leave? Who would visit them and comfort them, bring them word about the good things their Bahá'í brothers and sisters are doing around the world? They live for that.

MONA: So you need to die for it?

FATHER: Honey...

MONA: Do it for me if you won't do it for yourself!

FATHER: What can I say? My life is His, and He can take me.

MONA: So you want to die?

FATHER: No. But part of our Faith demands we change our attitude towards death. It is not the end, and we shouldn't fear it as such. What does Bahá'u'lláh say, "I have made death a messenger of joy to thee. Wherefore dost thou grieve?" So don't grieve, my sweet. (*Hugs her as she starts to break again.*) If it were mine to choose, you think I wouldn't want to be part of your life and see you grow and learn and flourish and marry?

MONA: (*Softly.*) But you can, can't you?

He doesn't answer.

MONA: (*Shaking her head.*) We just want to help, but these people— They have no souls.

FATHER: No, no, no, Mona. They have the very same soul, and the same possibility in their lives. Believe that, see that they are your sisters and brothers, but that they are in grave danger, moral danger.

MONA: It's one thing if they put themselves in danger, it's another if they put us, YOU, in danger.

FATHER: Do you think it's an accident that they target us? Or it's just because we're weak and an easy scapegoat? (*Shakes his head.*) We're a direct threat to them.

MONA: What?

FATHER: They're devoting every ounce of their might to forging a world with an imbalance of power, governed by fear, fueled by prejudice, fostered in a climate of ignorance. If there were no clash...

MONA: We wouldn't be doing our work.

FATHER: This is the test, isn't it? (*Pause.*) The world can change, but it will need some of us to stand and point the way.

MONA: So you can't leave.

FATHER: Don't despair. And don't lose hope in people. Transformation can happen to anyone, at any moment. So find the light in each one. Then you will rise from a creature of the earth to be a heavenly being. Then you will be a true Bahá'í.

ACT I, Scene 12 – The Ruins of the House of the Báb

MONA *stands straight and faces forward, with* FARAH *beside her. Both wear head scarves. The arches of a mosque are behind them.* ARAM *is there, and he looks anxious.*

MONA: You're sure you want to do this? Someone over here might come after us.

FARAH: (*Anxious.*) Why are we here again?

MONA: I come when I need strength. This is the House of the Báb. This is where my Faith began.

FARAH: I don't see what's controversial. There's nothing here.

MONA: Why else would they knock it down and leave no trace? (*Slight pause.*) Ready?

FARAH: (*Referring to* ARAM.) What about the guy?

MONA: He can come in if he'd like.

MONA *holds* FARAH'*s hand, closes her eyes a moment, and when she reopens them, she takes a step forward, toward the audience.*

ARAM: Hey!

MONA: He spoke.

FARAH: (*More quietly.*) You shouldn't go in there.

MONA: Go report me if you want.

MONA *walks in, followed by* FARAH. ARAM *is not pleased, and he walks off so as not to see what they are doing.*

MONA: So, in the front here was a wall about this tall—like those houses over there—with a door about here. There was a courtyard with the orange tree right there. (*Moving into the audience with* FARAH.) Windows all around, and a second floor with a flat roof. Up there with all the stained glass is the most important spot, where it all began.

MONA *seems to be seeing all she describes, but* FARAH'*s focus is on her friend, who seems to be changing before her very eyes.*

ACT I, Scene 13 – Mona's Home

Mona's MOTHER *sews distractedly. A knock.*

MOTHER: (*Anxiously stands.*) Come in.

MRS. KHUDAYAR: (*Opens the door, points to a newly-installed peephole.*) What is this, a peephole?

MOTHER: (*As if she's forgotten.*) Oh, in case someone comes. Some friends were just here, Jamshid let them install it—I guess to make them feel better.

MRS. KHUDAYAR: You should turn it around so I can see what's going on inside.

MOTHER: Yes, maybe.

MRS. KHUDAYAR: That was a joke. Look at you worried to death: What can I do?

MOTHER: What can anyone do? They're down there now begging him to go into hiding. There are rumors of arrests—My throat.

MRS. KHUDAYAR: We thought with the Shah gone, it would be freedom for everyone.

MOTHER: (*Sipping her tea.*) Excuse me for drinking.

MRS. KHUDAYAR: You know? I'm thirsty too.

MOTHER: I would offer…

MRS. KHUDAYAR: Okay.

The MOTHER *looks at her surprised.* MRS. KHUDAYAR *nods, though a bit uncertainly. The* MOTHER *then exits to the kitchen.*

MRS. KHUDAYAR: When they come, they're going to trash this place. What if I took your rug and some other things… to hide?

MOTHER: (*Enters, with tea.*) You don't need to do that.

MRS. KHUDAYAR: I insist.

ACT 1, SCENE 13

MRS. KHUDAYAR *takes the cup.* The MOTHER *watches it go to her lips where it stops.*

MRS. KHUDAYAR: Always they told me your tea was a magic potion. (*A slight pause.*) Please let me take some of your things.

MOTHER: Okay.

MRS. KHUDAYAR *takes a sip, and then pauses.*

MOTHER: Well?

MRS. KHUDAYAR: Well, I'm disappointed. It's just tea.

They laugh.

MRS. KHUDAYAR: Come on, let me get that son of mine to help in here.

ACT I, Scene 14 – The Mulla's Office

ARAM *is getting grilled by the* MULLA. GUARD 1 *watches.*

MULLA: But why didn't you report it yourself?

ARAM *is quiet.*

MULLA: Why did I have to hear that the girl and her friend were walking on that damned spot by someone else? That's why I have you! To tell me what they're doing. Not to make me look like an idiot when the guy who sits by the shoes and helps wash people's feet knows more about what the Bahá'ís are doing than I do! What do you have to say for yourself?

ARAM: I didn't think it was that important.

MULLA: It's not your place to think what's important. It's your place to come to me with everything you see and then I decide for you what is and what is not important! Got it?

ARAM *doesn't speak.*

MULLA: Now go get the truck, you've got a busy night tonight.

He exits. GUARD 1 *stops* ARAM *from leaving.*

GUARD 1: You know what this guy can do to you?

ACT I, Scene 15 – A Street near Mona's Home

It's evening. FARAH *is latched onto* MONA's *arm, and they now walk silently, knowing they need to part ways.*

FARAH: I'm not letting go. I'm worried.

MONA: Why?

FARAH: Sorry, all my friends have guard escorts.

MONA: (*Looking back.*) He seems to be gone. It's my father. They don't usually target women, much less girls like me—Don't be sad.

She squishes FARAH's *cheeks into a smile, but it doesn't stay.*

FARAH: You're changing, aren't you?

MONA: What do you mean?

FARAH: I just feel like you're starting to float away from me.

MONA: I'll always be here with you.

FARAH: Promise?

MONA: (*Smiles, looks up at the sky.*) Pick a star. (*Pause.*) See that bright star near the moon. Look at it and I'm right there with you.

FARAH *points to a star lower on the horizon.*

MONA: Good, that's yours for me.

They hug and part ways.

ACT I, Scene 16 – Mona's Home

The MOTHER *looks about the room that is now missing the rug and a couple of other things. The* FATHER *is then heard off stage talking to* MRS. KHUDAYAR.

FATHER: (*Off.*) Thank you so much, Thank you. I'm sorry, we'll just keep these things in here.

MRS. KHUDAYAR: (*Off, overlapping.*) I insist. Really, it's better we keep them.

MONA *enters, looking down the hall at her* FATHER *and* MRS. KHUDAYAR *playing tug of war.*

MONA: What's going on?

The MOTHER *shakes her head. The* FATHER *enters with the rug and the couple of others things.*

MOTHER: She was trying to be kind. (*Stopping him*) She drank some of our tea.

FATHER: So?

MOTHER: So the peephole didn't help us either. I thought you'd be proud of me.

MRS. KHUDAYAR: (*Entering.*) It's no problem.

MOTHER: It's just a rug…

FATHER: (*To his wife, at once gentle and firm.*) You think I care about the rug?

MONA *watches, in awe of her* FATHER *whose behavior is difficult to gauge sometimes.* REZA *is now at the door.*

FATHER: Let's say, just hypothetically, that Reza here were to ask for the hand of a girl like, say, Mona.

MONA *and* REZA *are both embarrassed by this.*

ACT 1, SCENE 16

MRS. KHUDAYAR: I've told him to get it out of his head—he's not good enough for you.

REZA: Mom!

FATHER: For example—and if he brought a beautiful engagement ring, just right: would he skimp on the box? It might cost a little extra.

MRS. KHUDAYAR: He better not—cheapskate.

FATHER: (*Takes his wife and daughter in his arms.*) These are my diamonds, and our home and everything in it is just a box.

MRS. KHUDAYAR: Of course.

REZA: (*Leaving, to his mother.*) Why do you have to embarrass me like that?

> MRS. KHUDAYAR *exits after him. The* FATHER *goes into the kitchen.*

MOTHER: I don't understand that man. Just when I think I do, he goes and changes all the rules on me. And I feel like a child. (*Turning to* MONA.) Even if they do come and arrest him, even if the worst comes. We'll be strong and we'll get through this, okay? If we stay united, we can do it, honey.

> MONA *comforts her* MOTHER. *Her* FATHER *has been watching this exchange from the doorway. He solemnly and gratefully nods and steps back out of sight.*

MOTHER: You hungry?

> MONA *nods. The* MOTHER *exits into the kitchen and passes by the* FATHER, *who now enters with a plate of food.*

FATHER: My dear, I didn't greet you properly. (*Kisses her and makes to share the plate with her.*)

MONA: You look tired.

FATHER: Thank you. You look radiant.

MONA: I should, I was at the House of the Bab.

FATHER: Mmmm. One day we'll rebuild. If not in my lifetime, then in yours.

MONA: Dad, you might just grow old in this world, and that way, you'll have to take better care of yourself. When I finish school this year, maybe we can look at colleges in other places. We can go to Africa, or America. What do you think?

FATHER: Have an olive.

He puts it in her mouth. A moment of tenderness before MONA *exits. The* MOTHER *has entered and sits beside her husband, affectionately close.*

MOTHER: Maybe she's right. You remember when the girls were young how we used to move so often, and every time you would go ahead and prepare the house, and you'd dress up in your best clothes and come and wait for me. And I'd arrive and you'd usher me in like a queen.

FATHER: I remember each time.

MOTHER: Maybe we'll do that again someday.

FATHER: No thanks.

They laugh. There is a sudden pounding on the door. MONA *is still offstage. Whirling in confusion, the* MOTHER *moves to the door.*

MOTHER: Maybe someone... just... has a question or something. Who is it?

GUARD: (*Off.*) Revolutionary Guard, open up!

MOTHER: (*Hushed.*) Oh, no!

The FATHER *closes his eyes and prepares himself.*

MRS. KHUDAYAR: (*Off.*) They're not home. Why don't you come back later?

MOTHER: It's Mrs. Khudayar...

GUARD 1: (*Off.*) Oh, I think they are home.

MRS. KHUDAYAR: (*Off.*) I saw them go out

One of the GUARDS *begin to force his weight against the door.*

MOTHER: I should have used the peephole! What do I do now?

FATHER: (*Rising.*) Open the door and let them in.

The MOTHER *puts on a dark chador and opens the door as the* FATHER *joins her. He is shaking slightly.*

FATHER: Good evening, friends. What can I do for you?

GUARD 2: We are from the Revolutionary Court. We have a warrant to enter.

GUARD 2 hands him the warrant. The FATHER *looks at it.*

FATHER: Please come in.

GUARDS 1 *and* 2 *enter brusquely, followed by* ARAM. *He looks around, surprised not to see* MONA.

GUARD 2: (*To* FATHER.) You sit there, (*To* MOTHER.) And you over there.

GUARD 1: Just you two? (*To* ARAM.) Check for the girl.

ARAM *looks, then* MONA *enters from the bathroom.*

MONA: You.

ARAM: Please go sit on the couch.

MOTHER: Mona, come sit.

GUARD 2: You be quiet.

MONA: I need to cover my hair. (*Moves towards her room.*)

GUARD 2: Come here, girl.

ARAM: Just go and sit down.

MONA: You are not my father and you're not my brother, so I have to cover my hair in your presence.

MONA *goes and gets a scarf around her hair, and retrieves a book.* ARAM *waits.*

GUARD 1: (*Looking through the father's papers.*) Get her out here, we don't have all night!

MONA *comes out, and* GUARD 2 *goes in and closes the door.*

ARAM: (*Low, to* MONA.) Sorry.

MONA *goes to the couch. Just then,* MRS. KHUDAYAR *pushes open the door.* REZA *follows sheepishly behind.*

MRS. KHUDAYAR: Excuse me?

ARAM: Hey, I need some backup in here!

MRS. KHUDAYAR: No trouble, I just want to help.

GUARD 2: Go back to your home!

MRS. KHUDAYAR: Sure, but maybe while you're searching, I can take them too.

GUARD 2: They are unclean!

MRS. KHUDAYAR: They're good people!

GUARD 2: Get out of here!

MRS. KHUDAYAR: Maybe I'm Bahá'í too!

GUARD 2: You don't know the first thing about it!

MRS. KHUDAYAR: How do you know?

GUARD 2: Because I read your mail and listen to your phone calls.

FATHER: (*Rising.*) Thank you so much. We'll let you know when they're done.

GUARD 1: What's going on? (*To* FATHER.) You sit down until we're ready. (*To* MRS. KHUDAYAR.) You, you want your son to go fight in Iraq?

GUARD 2 *levels his gun at* REZA, *who begins to tremble.*

MRS. KHUDAYAR: God no.

GUARD 1: Go home and lock the door.

MRS. KHUDAYAR *obeys, exits with* REZA. GUARD 1 *gives* ARAM *a look.*

GUARD 1: (*To* ARAM.) What's wrong with you?

ARAM: She just walked in.

GUARD 1: No one moves.

MOTHER: (*Shivering.*) Jamshid, they're going to take you.

The FATHER *has his eyes closed.* MONA *has a textbook open, but she's not reading it.* GUARDS 1 *and* 2 *overturn everything.* GUARD 2 *brings in a plastic bag full of Mona's writings and tapes.*

GUARD 1: We've got what we need. (*To* FATHER.) You and the girl, you're coming with us.

FATHER: The girl?

MONA: Me?

ACT 1, SCENE 16

FATHER: But why?

MOTHER: You've got to be kidding.

GUARD 1: We're not kidding.

MONA *stands with a mixture of shock and honor.* ARAM *grabs a black chador from a hook for* MONA, *but the* MOTHER *stops him.*

MOTHER: If you want to take my husband, okay! But Mona is just a child.

GUARD 2: The things she's writing? These tapes of her voice? They could set the world on fire.

GUARD 1: He means that she could lead others into the fire of ignorance.

MOTHER: All right then, take me instead!

MONA: Mom, calm down.

GUARD 2: Woman, we don't want you.

MOTHER: (*To* ARAM.) Swear to God you won't take her! You won't take her!

MONA: Mom, why are you begging them? I'm not a criminal. They're taking me because of my belief. (*To* GUARD 2.) I'll get my coat.

She goes into her destroyed room. Her FATHER *speaks to his wife.*

FATHER: Farkhundih. (*Looking into the men's faces.*) These men. I love these brothers like my own sons. I am sure it is the will of God that they are here now to take Mona and myself away with them. Just leave everything in God's hands and don't worry about Mona. These brothers look on Mona as their own sister.

The GUARDS *are taken in by this. The* FATHER *indicates he is ready and walks out with* GUARD 1. GUARD 2 *has thrown books, papers and photo albums on top of the carpet, and he rolls it up, indicating to* ARAM *to grab the other side.* ARAM *waits though on* MONA, *who has reentered with her coat.*

MOTHER: You look like a queen.

The MOTHER *takes the black veil from* ARAM *and helps* MONA *put it on. It wraps around and covers up all her color.*

MOTHER: (*Imploring* ARAM.) Tell me you won't take her. Ask the one in charge. No one will notice if she's doesn't go. She's just a girl...

GUARD 2 *is dragging the filled carpet off by himself. Only when he's gone does* ARAM *speak—quietly, dejectedly.*

ARAM: I'm sorry. There's nothing I can do.

MONA: (*Reassuring her* MOTHER.) Mom, it won't be a prison for me, but an open field, a mountain top where I can touch the moon. Please don't worry. We'll see you soon.

She kisses her MOTHER *and, as she goes to leave, she pulls out the blue dress and pushes it into* ARAM*'s hands without looking at him.* ARAM *then closes the door on the* MOTHER, *who is left alone.*

End of Act I

ACT II, Scene 1 – Prison; an interrogation room

MONA *stands blindfolded. She is refusing to answer questions in an interrogation led by* GUARD 2.

GUARD 2: Tired yet?

MONA *doesn't answer, but it's clear she is tired. She remains standing while the scene shifts to* FARAH, *who reads a letter from Mona in front of class. This is a bold move for* FARAH *and for the* TEACHER *to allow it.*

FARAH: "I put my trust in God to get this letter to you—and in Mínú who is smuggling it out! We're not supposed to write anything except for all the forms they try to get us to fill out. Forty Bahá'ís, both men and women, were arrested the same night. From what I can gather, I'm the youngest. But don't worry too much about me, I have a wonderful family here with my fellow women prisoners, both Bahá'ís and Muslims. (The Muslims call me 'little prisoner.') Last night, I felt as though I were on a balcony getting closer to the moon, but I kept seeing my mother's face. Farah, please go see her, and my sister and little Nura, and hug and kiss them for me. They visit, but there's a barrier between us. As for my father, I have only seen him once since coming here."

Scene shift away from the classroom and back to the Interrogation room. MONA'*s legs are asleep, and she winces to shake them out.*

GUARD 2: Answer me and I'll let you sit. Describe your Bahá'í activities.

No response.

GUARD 2: We can arrange your release.

Still no response.

GUARD 2: Look, I know this is more your parents' religion than yours.

ARAM *has entered and whispers to* GUARD 2.

GUARD 2: So what if I brought your father in here to persuade you to talk to me? *(Getting close.)* But you know your father wouldn't do that, right?

He nods to ARAM, *who exits.*

GUARD 2: He took many days, but since then, he's been quite useful to us.

MONA: You'll never break my father.

GUARD 2: No? I just broke you.

MONA *clams up. Mona's* FATHER *is wheeled in, blindfolded, ravaged by torture, having been whipped constantly on the back and on the feet. When he speaks, it's with a soft, strained voice.*

GUARD 2: Mahmudnizhad, your daughter is here.

FATHER: Mona dear?

MONA: Dad?

GUARD 2: Stay where you are. Tell her.

FATHER: Answer their questions, honey.

MONA *doesn't know how to respond.*

FATHER: Tell them what they want to know, Mona. Tell them the truth.

MONA: Dad, what have they done to you?

GUARD 2: You want to see?

YOUNG MAN: *(Quietly.)* Wait.

GUARD 2: What?

ARAM *objects, showing some backbone.*

GUARD 2: What, are you going soft? *(Continuing.)* Fine, just imagine the soles of his feet being struck with a rod time and again as the pain shoots up the body into the brain...

FATHER: *(Overlapping.)* You don't need to share this.

GUARD 2: Oh I do. You see it's cleaner than the back lashes, because you know it takes several days for the feet to start to bleed. But when they do, they bleed from the nails.

MONA: What makes you people so sick?

GUARD 2: See, you've got it upside down. You are sick, and we resort to these means to cure you!

FATHER: Mona, after a while I don't feel the pain.

MONA: But the agreement!

A beat, while the FATHER *gathers the strength to speak.*

FATHER: We have no secrets, Mona. Our activities are not political, and we are faithful to our country.

GUARD 2: So your world center in Israel isn't political!

FATHER: (*Matter-of-factly.*) You exiled our Prophet there a hundred years ago, locked Him in a stone fortress. Where else is our world center going to be?

GUARD 2: (*To* ARAM.) Hit him!

ARAM: You want me to get 'Abdu'lláh?

GUARD 2: No I want you to hit him.

MONA: Don't.

GUARD 2: Shut up! It's either him or her.

MONA: Me then.

FATHER: Please.

MONA: (*To* ARAM.) You can stand up to them—tell them this is not the way of Islam.

GUARD 2: Don't tell me about Islam. (*To* ARAM, *as if it's his last chance.*) Hit him or I tell the Magistrate.

ARAM *picks up the whip, and then picks up the Qur'án, which lies open. He puts the book under his arm (a practice employed to limit the force of the lashes).*

GUARD 2: What are you doing?

ARAM: To get the right amount of force.

GUARD 2: This man is an apostate—you hit him like this, this is going to save him from the fires of hell?!

ARAM: Okay!

ARAM *begins to whip the* FATHER's *back.* MONA *is torn.*

FATHER: Mmmm.

GUARD 2: Harder! Girl?

Another lash.

FATHER: Aaaah!

GUARD 2: Again, harder! GIIRRLL?

Another lash.

FATHER: Yá Bahá'u'l-abhá!

MONA: STOP!

GUARD 2: Are you going to talk?!

MONA: (*After a pause.*) Let me see his eyes...

GUARD 2 *senses victory and motions to* ARAM, *who pulls up his mask, then takes off their blindfolds.* MONA *goes to her* FATHER.

MONA: Oh Dad! Look at you ...

FATHER: Is it really you?

MONA: What have they done?

FATHER: Don't look there—let me see you.

They look in each other's eyes.

GUARD 2: Tell her.

FATHER: Answer them bravely and honestly. We have nothing to hide.

MONA *hesitates.*

GUARD 2: Quick, quick.

FATHER: Tell the women to see their captors not as enemies but as friends, with whom they can share their love.

MONA: What?

GUARD 2: He thinks he's going to convert us!

MONA: But is that right?

FATHER: Do I look like I have any secrets left?

ACT 2, SCENE 1

A beat in which MONA *seems to assent.*

GUARD 2: Let me get the Magistrate.

He exits. MONA *looks at her father's wounds.*

MONA: They're not friends. They're devils.

FATHER: Don't hate them. Don't even be angry with them.

ARAM *is there.*

MONA: (*Gives him an evil look.*) Leave us alone.

ARAM: Sir, I'm sorry.

FATHER: Son, it was more painful for you.

ARAM *is moved.* MONA *is livid.*

MONA: How can you say that?

ARAM: (*Still to* FATHER.) I'm going to make sure she's released, okay?

MONA: I don't want anything from you, just stay away!

FATHER: Love, Mona. Only love.

MONA is speechless, unable to fathom this depth. ARAM *starts to push the* FATHER *out one of the doors. In a vision,* MONA *sees the* WOMAN IN WHITE *at the door, radiant, watching the* FATHER *wheeled off. Then, the door opposite opens and fire seems to pour in.* MONA *hides her face just as the* MULLA *enters. He looks at* MONA *curiously.*

MULLA: Where's her blindfold?

GUARD 2: She has all the forms to answer.

MONA has opened her eyes, but she keeps her gaze averted.

MULLA: (*To* MONA.) Sweetheart, we're going to let you go. Don't worry, we just need you to do a little paperwork.

He looks her over and raises his eyebrows to GUARD 2. *He then walks out.* GUARD 2 *hands* MONA *a stack of papers and a pen. The air returns to the room and she settles in to the burden of paperwork.*

ACT II, Scene 2 – A Prison Office

TARANEH *and* MOTHER *approach the front entrance to the prison.* TARANEH *carries a baby girl, little* NURA. *The* MOTHER *has Mona's release paper in her hand.*

MOTHER: I'm telling you there are no gas stations out here.

TARANEH: We'll walk back! I'm not going to miss getting Mona.

MOTHER: It's not a sure thing they'll release her, form or no form.

TARANEH: (*Bangs on the door.*) Hello, we have a visit scheduled! (*To* MOTHER.) So you have the money?

MOTHER: (*Referring to baby.*) I can't believe the way she slept.

TARANEH: She's used to Mommy's driving. The Assembly agreed to the bond, right? (*Bangs on the door again.*) Hey, it's one o'clock!

The MOTHER *appears not to have heard her question.*

TARANEH: Mom?

MOTHER: Sorry, I can't concentrate now. I'm so worried about them both.

TARANEH: (*Suspicious, takes the paper from her* MOTHER.) So first we visit with Mona and then they release her? That doesn't make sense.

MOTHER: (*Hands on her kidneys.*) Aaaeeeee.

GUARD 1 *comes to open the door.*

MOTHER: Is it possible to come in? I'd like to freshen up before my visit, you understand.

GUARD 1: Just you.

MOTHER: This is her sister.

GUARD 1: She needs to wait outside.

ACT 2, SCENE 2

TARANEH: Go ahead, Mom. I'll... I'll just wait out here.

She hands the release to her MOTHER *and walks off with the baby. The* MOTHER *is ushered into an office by* GUARD 1.

GUARD 1: It'll be another minute.

MOTHER: Is it possible to freshen up before my visit, you understand?

GUARD 1: It'll just be a minute.

He is gone. She tries to sit.

MOTHER: (*Hands on her kidneys.*) Ooohhhhhh. (*She is back up.*) O God, I want my child. I want Mona from you. I want to touch her, to kiss her cheek. The little birds all fly free but my little bird is trapped in a cage. O God, we need a miracle. Bring her to me.

The MULLA *enters.*

MULLA: Please sit.

MOTHER: Please, is there a rest room?

MULLA: I'll make this quick if you will.

ARAM *enters.*

MULLA: Where's the girl's file?

ARAM *has forgotten this, and exits, embarrassed. The* MOTHER *goes to hand the release paper to the* MULLA.

MULLA: So what was it, 100,000 Tuman?

MOTHER: (*Hesitates with the form.*) Something like that—

MULLA: (*Overlapping, snatching the form from her.*) It was 200, I remember.

MOTHER: Can I see her now?

MULLA: Can I see the money?

MOTHER: There is concern if we pay 200,000 now, tomorrow it might be 400, the next day 600.

MULLA: You think I'm going to cheat you?

MOTHER: Not me, if it were just me...

MULLA: Who then? The Bahá'í Assembly?

MOTHER: You're twisting my words.

ARAM reenters with a thick stack of papers.

MULLA: *(To* ARAM.*)* It's all here?

ARAM *nods.*

MULLA: And where is she?

ARAM: She's in a holding room, just down the hall here.

MOTHER: She's right here. Please let me see her. Just say you won't increase bail, I'll pay you in 24 hours.

A beat. The MULLA *calculates.*

MULLA: *(To* ARAM.*)* Send the girl back to her cell. *(Hands* ARAM *the release form. To* MOTHER.*)* Now I have some questions for you.

Flustered, ARAM *goes into the hall and he lingers there, looks at the form. The* MOTHER *is disbelieving.*

MULLA: Who made this decision about the bail?

MOTHER: What more do you need from me? You have my husband, you have my daughter. Maybe I have a few questions for you.

MULLA: I want names.

MOTHER: I'm not your prisoner.

MULLA: No?

He impulsively takes a stamp and brings it down on a legal form, then signs it.

MULLA: Now you're my prisoner. *(Gets up to go.)* You think you can toy with me, woman.

He walks out to the hall and sees ARAM *there. The* MOTHER *is aghast.*

MULLA: *(Impatient.)* What?

ARAM: *(Holding Mona's release.)* You said you want me to put her back in her cell?

MULLA: You want to toy with me too, boy? *(Tears the release in two, tosses it in the air.)* No, no, no, this is all going to change!

He exits. ARAM *picks up the torn release form. Seeing the devastated* MOTHER, *he follows after the Mulla, stealthily, as if to spy on him.*

ACT II, Scene 3 – A Prison Holding Room

MONA *waits. The sound of screaming from doors down. The door opens; it's* ARAM. *He looks around, makes a judgment, shuts the door and locks it.*

MONA: (*Nervous.*) A woman needs to be here.

ARAM: We need to talk.

MONA: Am I being released?

ARAM: No.

MONA: Then take me to my cell.

ARAM: I just overheard something: he's going to start executing women.

> MONA *sits. He takes out a pen and the torn release, which he has taped.*

MONA: What's that for?

ARAM: If you just write down a few sentences, I think they'll let you go.

MONA: Please take me back to my cell.

ARAM: It's just a piece of paper. (*A beat.*) Look, I've been watching you, and your father, and others. I know it's not right. I know you're good people. But if you let them do this, out of pride or spite or whatever it is that makes you people so stubborn, you are responsible, Mona.

> *A beat.*

MONA: (*Still cold.*) What's your name?

ARAM: Aram.

MONA: (*Maybe not fully believing.*) If they kill us, Aram, God will raise up others greater than us.

ARAM: You don't know that.

MONA: I do. That's how it works.

Someone bangs on the door. ARAM *jumps back behind where the door would open.*

ARAM: (*Whispers.*) Hide.

MONA *doesn't. Someone checks the door, finds it locked, and passes.* ARAM *comes back to the table.*

ARAM: You had a dream, with the dresses.

MONA: (*Defenses rising.*) You read my file?

ARAM: (*Not flinching.*) Doesn't it make sense that I am here in front of you, apparently chosen by God, to remind you what He has chosen for you? Not death, not suffering, but life.

ARAM *has written something on the paper and pushes it towards her.*

MONA: (*Reading.*) "I renounce my membership in the Bahá'í Faith." (*Pauses.*) Here's the truth: I chose the blue dress and I served. I chose the black and I've suffered. As for the red, I don't know if I am ready or worthy, but if you're the face I saw, it's not because you're chosen of God, but it's that, despite the terrible, terrible things you've done, I have to stop hating you!

She rips up the release paper and throws it in the air.

ARAM: Terrible things like what?

MONA: Like killing Ehsan, Mr. Khushkhu, and Mr. Vahdat.

ARAM: No. Your friend, he kissed my hand. I couldn't fire, but I watched him die, like a hero, and now he haunts me every waking moment, following me wherever I go. I never killed anyone.

ARAM *doesn't see that the door has been opened, and the* MULLA *stands, keys in hand, listening to all this.*

MULLA: Is that right?

ACT II, Scene 4 – Outside the Prison

TARANEH *bangs on the same door as before, little* NURA *sleeping in her arms. She bangs harder.* GUARD 1 *comes out.*

GUARD 1: We're closed.

TARANEH: Sorry, I've been waiting for my mother. Do you know where she is?

GUARD 1: No. Come back tomorrow. (*Goes to leave.*)

TARANEH: I don't have enough gas to get home, my mother has our cash. Can you go back inside and ask for her?

GUARD 1: No.

He leaves. TARANEH *is stunned.*

GUARD 1: (*To sleeping daughter.*) What do we do now, sweetie? (*A beat.*) I was in such a rush.

GUARD 1 *reenters. He opens the door, pushes some money (5 tuman) into her hand, then goes.*

TARANEH: Thank you—God.

ACT II, Scene 5 – Prison Courtyard

It's night. MONA *and several other women are blindfolded in a staggered line. The* MULLA *is there with a machine gun in his hand as he remonstrates with* ARAM. GUARD 2 *is nearby with a gun of his own.*

MULLA: So why the Revolutionary Guard, Hafez, if you lack the constitution for it? And be honest, a general needs to know where his soldiers stand.

ARAM: I preferred Shiraz to Iraq.

MULLA: Well, that's honest. Shiraz sure beats Iraq! (*Laughs.*) Yeah, but you know, wherever you go, God will find you out. (*Hands him the gun. Speaks to* GUARD 2.) Get 'em lined up.

GUARD 2: Prisoners! Line up, and stand up straight!

The MULLA *nods and* GUARD 2 *raises his gun, aiming at the women.* ARAM *hesitates to do the same, so the* MULLA *indicates to* GUARD 2 *to level his gun at* ARAM. ARAM *raises his gun tepidly.*

MULLA: Ladies, you are about to be executed. See if your Bahá'í God saves you now.

Some begin to cry and pray aloud. MONA *squeezes the hand of the woman next to her.*

MONA: God help us.

The MULLA *nods to* ARAM *to fire.* ARAM *can't. Instead* GUARD 2 *begins to fire wildly. Screams and bodies falling and writhing.* ARAM *looks on, stunned, to see perhaps half of the women who remain standing as if nothing has touched them.*

A scene shift where the WOMAN IN WHITE *appears, luminous, as if a protector of these several women. A celestial birdsong.*

ACT 2, SCENE 5

The women look around, blindfolds still on. Are they dead? Moaning is heard, then weeping. The cries come mainly from the ones who have fallen. One begins to rage.

WOMAN: We're alive! They didn't shoot—this is just a sick, twisted game!

ARAM *is just as shocked as the women.* GUARD 2 *though was in the know.*

GUARD 2: (*Smiles, to* ARAM.) Aimed over their heads.

ARAM *catches his breath.*

MULLA: They weren't the real target. (*Takes* ARAM*'s gun. To* GUARD 2.) Take the ones on the ground to interrogation. The ones standing, bring them to their cells. (*To* MONA*'s group.*) Congratulations, ladies, you won that round. Miss Mahmudnizhad, you'll be happy to know your mother will be waiting for you.

MONA: My mother?

She and the other are ushered off. The MULLA *and* ARAM *are left.*

MULLA: (*With a mixture of admiration and impatience.*) See that? When they don't fear death any more, we start to run out of options. And then there are things worse than death, right, Hafez?

ACT II, Scene 6 – Prison Cell & Visitation Area

MONA *is brought to her cell with* WOMAN 2, *one of those who remained standing in the previous scene. Their blindfolds are removed.*

MONA: Did you see it?

WOMAN 2 *nods in wonder.*

MONA: It was like a world of love and light opening up to us. I don't know why we're still here.

They comfort each other. Her MOTHER *is brought in. She is layered with blankets.* WOMAN 2 *is led off.*

MOTHER: Mona? Is that you?

MONA: Mom?

MOTHER: Oh honey, I love you so much. Oh, let me hug you, let me kiss you!

MONA: What are you doing in here?

MOTHER: They kept me in that room for hours! It was awful. But what's happened to you? Look at you, you're shaking?

MONA: I'm just so happy to see you.

They hold each other tight. Scene shift to the Visitation Area. The FATHER *and* TARANEH *are separated by a glass barrier and they speak through phones.*

TARANEH: You know Mom is in now.

He nods. TARANEH *begins to cry. He shakes his head.*

FATHER: It's not as bad as that.

TARANEH: Dad, I just feel so helpless and alone. I can't seem to do anything to get you released. I try: I go here, they send me there, I go there, they send me right back. I'm depressed and it's not good for the baby, I know. I feel...

FATHER: What?

TARANEH: I feel left out, like God has forgotten me. Wasn't I worth being imprisoned for my Faith too?

FATHER: My dear, you on the outside are in the harsher prison.

TARANEH: (*Nodding, then—*) You mean Iran?

He smiles lovingly. The scene shifts back to the prison cell, where MONA, *her* MOTHER, *and a couple other women sit back to back on the ground.*

MOTHER: Here, honey, take a blanket. I just threw them all on top of me.

MONA: I'm okay. Have you eaten yet?

MOTHER: So cold in here! I don't know how you girls aren't freezing to death.

MONA: Here, Mom, have another blanket. You haven't eaten your dinner.

MOTHER: I don't know who could. And the smell, I can barely breathe.

MONA: You're just not used to it.

MOTHER: You get used to it?

MONA: It's important to keep the right attitude in here—

An obnoxiously loud VOICE *comes over the* P.A. *system.*

VOICE OVER P.A.: Prisoners! A victory for Islam! Last night, a husband and wife, recanted the Baháʼí heresy. Now they are free!

Someone groans. The rest seem to hold their breath.

VOICE OVER P.A.: To celebrate, we are letting family members in prison meet to talk it over.

Reactions. The other women kiss MONA *and her* MOTHER *and exit, as if back to their own cells.*

VOICE OVER P.A.: Islam is the open door!

The FATHER *makes his way, barely able to walk, but* GUARD 2 *helps him. He focuses ahead, trying not to give attention to the great pain, and sees* MONA *and the* MOTHER.

FATHER: Look, look who—Brother, thank you for bringing me this far.

MOTHER: O Lord!

MONA: Daddy!

MOTHER: Look at you, Jamshid. Look at what they've done to you.

Arriving, he shakes GUARD 2's *shoulders as if to show he is his brother.* MONA *and the* MOTHER *make room for him to sit, and for a while they just look at each other.*

MONA: You look like a candle.

FATHER: Just waiting for His breath to blow.

MOTHER: No, don't say that—you'll still be okay. Jamshid, what will become of me if you go?

FATHER: (*Speaking with difficulty, but with dignity and joy.*) My wife, from Bahá'u'lláh, our inheritance is prison. From the Báb, martyrdom.

MOTHER: Please stop—My heart is breaking.

FATHER: Mine is overflowing.

MONA *rises and kisses her* FATHER's *eyes. They look at each other and tears are falling.*

FATHER: I'm so happy. These tears are from happiness. This is not goodbye. We have a new home, I am going.

They MOTHER *is overcome, but she nods.*

FATHER: And when the time is right, I will come for you.

MOTHER: I'm going to hold you to that. I'm sorry, I'm so sorry …

FATHER: No, no. All is washed clean.

MOTHER: Please no more. Talk to Mona, you haven't said a word.

He looks into MONA's *eyes lovingly, searchingly.*

FATHER: Are you heavenly or earthly?

MONA: Heavenly.

FATHER: (*Standing with a spurt of energy.*) Then let's go!

Scene shift as if the FATHER *has started his ascent to the next world, embodied by the* WOMAN IN WHITE*'s beckoning.* MONA *sees and speaks to her* FATHER *as if across time, but the* MOTHER *recedes.* GUARD 2 *has entered.*

GUARD 2: Yadu'lláh Mahmúdni<u>zh</u>ád.

MONA: Must you go now?

GUARD 2: Rahmatu'lláh Vafáí.

FATHER: This separation is only temporary.

GUARD 2: Túbá Zá'irpúr

MONA: Just a little longer.

WOMAN IN WHITE: Come.

MONA: Wait. What about me?

FATHER: Your dress isn't finished. It should be one color, just one.

MONA: What do you mean?

FATHER: Love, Mona—This is the real color of your dress.

MONA: Daddy...!

The FATHER *goes with the* WOMAN IN WHITE. *We see, if anything, the briefest enactment in silence of the hanging of the three.*

FATHER: (*Just before going.*) May my life be sacrificed for you.

Silence.

MONA: (*Alone, without a tear.*) Won't you congratulate me, friends? My father has been martyred for his faith, and I am so immensely proud of him.

The silence is broken by the scream of the MOTHER, *who wanders just offstage, inconsolable, banging on the bars.*

MOTHER: (*Barely intelligible.*) Where is Mona? Where is my daughter?

MONA: (*Not addressing her directly, still with minimal emotion.*) Mother, I think I need to be alone.

ACT II, Scene 7 – Prison Cell and Elsewhere

It's the next night. MONA *is on the floor of their cell, facing away, praying fervidly. Her* MOTHER, *still grief-stricken, is comforted by other prisoners.*

MOTHER: It's been a full day: she doesn't eat, she doesn't talk. O God, I can't lose her too.

YOUNG MAN: Let her be. Come, Farkhundih, she'll be okay.

They move her off. Elsewhere, FARAH *is searching the sky for Mona's star.*

FARAH: Where are you tonight, Mona? I can't find your star. Are you up there? It's me, Farah. See me, on the horizon—there, at the foot of the bear. I look up, I see the moon, but no Mona nearby. You said you'd be there! Maybe the moon has swallowed you up, swallowed you whole, you made it jealous the way you shine. Can the moon put out the light of a star? No, I know this much: next to a star, a moon is a speck of dust. You'll come back. I'm counting on you to come back.

Scene shift back to MONA. *The prison though has shifted. There's no one around, no sound, and there are hints in the lighting that eternity waits behind these walls.* MONA *stands. She walks to the wall and kicks it.*

MONA: Let me out!

She shouts and hits the walls with her fists and feet.

MONA: (*More in pain than anger.*) I want out. Why don't you take me? You showed me the other side...Why am I still here where one pointless day leads into another unless for some reason? Does my pain mean anything? Does it...

She can't finish the thought. ARAM *is there in the shadows.*

ARAM: Say it.

MONA: (*Startled.*) What are you doing here?

ARAM: (*Finishing* MONA*'s thought.*) Does it please Him to see you in pain?

He has come more into the light; he is a wreck of abuse and wears a mask. He is weak and leans against a wall to keep balance.

ARAM: That's what you can't bring yourself to say.

MONA: You don't belong here.

The crack of a whip and ARAM *buckles. He lurches closer, struggling here and throughout to stand upright.*

MONA: Stop! Stay back!

ARAM: <u>You</u> need to stop!

MONA: (*Pushing back at him.*) Me?! You're threatening me!

Another crack of a whip.

ARAM: (*Falling back from her.*) Look at me!

ARAM *takes off his mask; his face is beaten black and blue. He struggles to stand upright.*

MONA: (*Repulsed.*) Yagghh...

ARAM: Look at what you did!

MONA: I didn't do that. Help!!

The WOMAN IN WHITE *is revealed with several other* SPIRITS.

WOMAN IN WHITE: Aram.

ARAM *goes to her, as if seeking her protection.*

WOMAN IN WHITE: Oooh...

She touches his face and looks to MONA, *who is astonished. Sensing she's being blamed,* MONA *shakes her head "no." The* WOMAN IN WHITE *smiles gently. There is a surging of light from beyond the prison walls. The* WOMAN IN WHITE *and the others turn towards the light.*

MONA: Are you here to take me? To where you are?

WOMAN IN WHITE: I'm here with you.

MONA: But you're not. You're... illumined.

WOMAN IN WHITE: This is the world of light.

There is another surging of light, brighter than before.

MONA: Then why is he here?

The whip again.

ARAM: Stop hurting me!

MONA: (*Advancing on him.*) You're the guard, you're the man—even though you have no spine...

The whip punctuates each statement.

ARAM: (*In agony.*) She's doing it again!

Overcome, he's attended to by the SPIRITS.

MONA: I don't understand.

WOMAN IN WHITE: The rules are different here. (*A beat.*) What is it that you want?

MONA: (*Bracing herself.*) I would like to trade my blue and black dresses for the red.

ARAM: (*Comes up to her.*) No! No! You can't!!

MONA: Do it!

She opens her arms as if bracing for death, but he doesn't touch her. Instead, the WOMAN IN WHITE *does.*

WOMAN IN WHITE: Mona, he can't hurt you here. Here you are strong.

The lights swell again. The MULLA *is wheeled across the back of the stage in a lamentable, comatose state. All turn to watch as mourners would a coffin.*

MONA: (*With awakened anxiety.*) So this is the next world? Why does it look like a prison?

WOMAN IN WHITE: (*Smiles gently.*) Friends...

She motions the SPIRITS *over. They gather around* MONA *as the prisoners had earlier. Silence as they listen.*

SPIRITS: (*Speaking alternately.*) Flowers. Air, fresh air. Sky. Water. Kebab.

They laugh.

SPIRITS: Love. Family. Companionship. Children (*All together.*) Children! (*One by one, again—*) She loves children.

ACT 2, SCENE 7

MONA *laughs.*

SPIRITS: Healing. Peace. Freedom. (*Several agree.*) Freedom.

MONA: (*Thrilled but anxious.*) But how is love for flowers or children or freedom bad?

The SPIRITS *resume listening, and only speak with reticence. They do not wish to look at the negative and are careful to mitigate.*

SPIRITS: Some fear. Anger. Often overcome through prayer. Need for justice. Retribution.

MONA: So is it a bad thing to want justice?

No response.

MONA: Come on, look what they've done. (*moved, tears*) They killed him. O God, they killed him, and now I can't see him anymore unless you let me come here.

SPIRITS: (*So gently.*) Heartbreak.

ARAM: It's despair.

He comes forward. The SPIRITS *do not object, but withdraw from the discussion. This is the darkness.*

ARAM: Despair that you are forgotten. And that even if God is there, He doesn't care about your pain. So to save yourself you kick and scream and flail at the night.

MONA: You see that in me?

ARAM: I see it in everyone. I try to avoid it, but, in my heart, I don't feel Him.

MONA: I do.

ARAM: Even when you look at me? (*A beat.*) God can work through me too, right, Mona? You're so... beyond where I am. If you don't see any hope for me...

He gestures "how can I?" but in such an innocent, childlike way. MONA *breathes in, and there is a crack and the prison walls begin to move. The light starts to shine in.*

ARAM: My father showed you such kindness, and I didn't understand. I saw what you'd done in darkness. He saw who you are, here.

WOMAN IN WHITE: It's time.

MONA: I'm not ready to go back. I don't know if I'll be able to hold onto this.

The vision is nearing an end as the light has reached its peak. ARAM *stands, more sturdily than before. Someone comes forward with a package. It has a red bow.*

WOMAN IN WHITE: What is it that you want?

MONA: (*After a moment.*) Perseverance.

The SPIRITS *gather around.*

WOMAN IN WHITE & SPIRITS: What do you want for yourself from us?

MONA: Perseverance for all the Bahá'ís.

WOMAN IN WHITE: What do you want for yourself from us?

The scene is painfully shifting back to the physical realm, back to the prison cell.

MONA: (*Under the strain of reentry.*) Perseverance, perseverance, perseverance.

WOMAN IN WHITE: We will be watching.

She is gone with her companions. It is now morning. MONA *sits on the bed, bathing in the light of a new day as it pours through an upstage window. Everywhere else is dark.*

The MOTHER *wakens to see* MONA *looking like a vision in light.*

MOTHER: How radiant you are.

MONA *turns and smiles.*

MOTHER: So you're back?

MONA *turns back to the light. The* MOTHER *sits on the bed.*

MOTHER: I've been trying to imagine life without your father, and all I can think of is how I want us to be free and you to have a family.

MONA: I need to tell you something.

MOTHER: Okay.

MONA: I'm going to be executed.

MOTHER: Don't say that.

MONA: Do you want to know how I know?

MOTHER: I don't want to know anything about that!

MONA: If you don't let me tell you, you will regret it later.

MOTHER: O God, you know a mother's heart, you created it and you see it breaking, don't you? Please don't let Mona be executed, please don't—

MONA: Mom, stop.

MOTHER: Look how beautiful you are. You can't see, but my God! If you died, don't you see what a pity it would be?

MONA: That's okay.

MOTHER: But a family! A loving husband! Children!

MONA: (*A discovery:*) Maybe a family is not what I want or need. (*Pauses, more discoveries:*) What I really want is bigger than that. I want to see this world changed, Mom. I want freedom and love and opportunity and joy and light for all the people of the world. And I want the children and the youth to take the lead. If they rose up and overcame the barriers that have separated us, if they learned to meet hatred with love, they could become a new race of men that the world has been waiting for, dying for! The world needs them, desperately, and I believe somehow, if I am strong enough to take this path before me, it will help them on their path. And they'll change this earth into heaven. That's what I want really. That's my dream, Mom. And for that dream, I wish I had a thousand lives to give. (*Pauses.*) Do you see?

The MOTHER *is changed by* MONA*'s vision.*

MOTHER: I do.

MONA *smiles.*

MOTHER: It frightens me, but I do. (*Standing up.*) If only they would come now and take us all!

GUARD 2 *enters.*

GUARD 2: It's time.

ACT II, Scene 8 – Prison Courtroom

A makeshift courtroom. The MULLA *sits at a large table. At the corner are a chair and a typewriter. There is a chair in front of the table meant for the accused.* GUARD 1 *leads the* MOTHER *forward.*

GUARD 1: Wait there, please. (*He takes up a seat before the typewriter.*) Come now.

The MOTHER *comes forward.*

MOTHER: Hello.

GUARD 1 *types it ('hello'). The* MOTHER *goes to the chair but doesn't sit down; instead she stands with her hand on the chair and pretends to be deaf.*

MULLA: Sit down, please.

MOTHER: What's that?

MULLA: Sit down.

MOTHER: Sorry?

MULLA: (*Smiling.*) So now you're deaf? (*To* GUARD 1.) This is the wife of the man who kept saying they have to tell the truth.

He laughs, and goes through her file. The MOTHER *is edified and gives up the deaf pretense.*

MOTHER: Is this all? I've seen courtrooms and hearings at the movies, and there is always a defense attorney and witnesses.

MULLA: This is not the movies! Sit down.

She does.

MULLA: You are from a Zoroastrian background, right?

MOTHER: Yes.

MULLA: Why did you leave such a good religion as the Faith of Zoroaster and convert to Bahá'ísm?

MOTHER: Because it was my heart's desire to do that.

MULLA: This is not a matter of the heart! If right now you declare you are Zoroastrian, I will set you free.

MOTHER: No sir, I will neither become a Zoroastrian nor a Muslim, so what is my sentence?

MULLA: Death.

MOTHER: *(Defiant.)* I am not worthy of martyrdom, but it would make me very happy. As God is my witness, it will make me immeasurably happy.

MULLA: You will be happy?

MOTHER: Yes.

MULLA: We are not here to make you happy! Take her.

The MOTHER *is taken away.* MONA *is brought in. Same business as before.*

MULLA: Your parents have deceived and misled you. They have forced you to imitate them.

MONA: It's true that I was born into it, but I have made up my own mind.

MULLA: Girl, you don't know the first thing about religion.

MONA *raises her gaze, which until now was lowered, and smiles.*

MULLA: Why are you smiling?

MONA: What more proof do you want? You took me out of my parents' home, out of school, brought me to this prison, put me through these interrogation and hardship, you killed my father—what haven't I suffered for my religion.

MULLA: Stop. Stop moving your arms and body like that—you're trying to distract me from my duties! *(A beat.)* What harm did you find in Islam that made you turn away from it?

MONA: I believe in Islam. I also believe that from time to time God renews His religion when it becomes darkened—and so He has sent a new Messenger, Bahá'u'lláh, and He has brought new laws...

MULLA: Muhammad is the Seal of the Prophets—There will be no more Messengers!

MONA: (*Overlapping.*) Now if by Islam you mean the hatred and bloodshed going on in this country, now that is the reason I'm a Bahá'í!

MULLA: Silence! (*Pause.*) We must obey the Qur'an. Accept Islam or face execution.

MONA: (*Moved.*) I kiss the order of execution.

MULLA: Very well, bring the mother back in!

GUARD 1 *exits. A bird is heard singing outside.*

MULLA: You're smiling again!

MONA: The world is waking up.

MULLA: Forget about the world! No one's going to hear what's happened to you here! It all ends right now. We're going to snuff you out—not just you, all of you! Somebody find that bird and kill it.

The MULLA *tries to regain his composure, calculates.* GUARD 1 *returns, leading the* MOTHER *in.* MONA *and her* MOTHER *stand side by side and hold hands in solidarity.*

MULLA: (*To* MOTHER.) Mrs. Mahmúdnizhád, you wanted to know what your sentence was?

MOTHER: Yes.

MULLA: We have killed your husband, we will now kill your daughter. Your sentence is your freedom. You are free to go home and spend the rest of your days mourning their loss.

This was unexpected.

MOTHER: Mona?

MONA: No tears, Mom, remember our talk!

MULLA: Get her out of here!

MOTHER: O my lovely daughter!

The MOTHER *is forced out of the room. The* MULLA *speaks to* GUARD 2, *referring to* MONA.

MULLA: Take her, put her with the other nine. Hang them one at a time from oldest to youngest. This one will be the last. Perhaps the sight of the older ones choking and flailing about will encourage the younger ones.

All are gone. The MULLA *sighs.*

Scene shift to a solitary confinement cell, the size of a dog cage. ARAM *is in it, though we can't recognize him at first. He whines like an animal. The* MULLA *comes up and crouches down.*

MULLA: I have a job for you if you're ready to come out.

He sticks his hand close to the bars, and ARAM *crawls to kiss it.*

ACT II, Scene 9 – An Abandoned Polo Field & Beyond

MONA *stands still, praying.* ARAM *enters, masked, bruised and beaten all over. He approaches* MONA.

ARAM: I don't want to kill you, Mona.

MONA: (*Without looking at him.*) Do your job.

ARAM: (*Takes off his mask.*) I had a vision of you, in my cell.

MONA: I'm sorry.

ARAM: You were nursing my wounds.

Something inside MONA *lets go. She looks up at* ARAM *with great love. Her* FATHER *and the* WOMAN IN WHITE *are now present.* MONA *takes* ARAM*'s hand, which he pulls back, but she gently insists.*

MONA: I see why now. You have made my dream come true.

ARAM: I'll tell them what you've done here.

She kisses his hand and they step upstage. The company comes forward to lay down dresses for each of the 10 women martyrs of Shiraz, as the actor playing the FATHER *reads their names.*

FATHER: 'Izzat Ishráqí. Nusrat Yaldá'í. Táhirih Síyávushí. Zarrín Muqímí. Mahshíd Nírúmand. Shírín Dálvand. Símín Sábirí. Akhtar Sábet. Royá Ishráqí. Mona Mahmúdnizhád.

When called, MONA *comes forward wearing the red dress and lays down her chador as the final dress.*

End of Play

Mona & Yadu'lláh Mahmúdnizhád

BAND OF GOLD

A play about Marriage, Family and Community

To an unfinished work: the Bahá'í community

To

Christian

Emily

Gordon

Leland

Leonard

Louise

Marda

Norma

Paul

And to

Gertrude,

the matron saint of Tampa

Setting

Palm Terrace, Florida (Near Tampa). 2006.

	Page
ACT I, Scene 1...The Jennison home. Evening of April 21	87
ACT I, Scene 2...The Sobhani home. Afternoon of April 22	122
ACT II, Scene 1...The Sobhani home. Evening of April 22	148
ACT II, Scene 2..The Jennison & Sobhani homes. Midnight, April 22	160
ACT II, Scene 3...The Sobhani home. A Saturday afternoon in July	179

Cast of Characters
(In order of appearance)

Melinda Jennison	40s, female, white American
Hal Jennison	40s, male, white American
Chris "Semowa" Manteha	21, male, biracial / African-American
Chadwick Alston	20s, male, African-American
Táhirih Sobhani	22, female, Persian-American *
Mr. (Sírús) Sobhání **	50s, male, Persian *
Mrs. (Parvín) Sobhání **	late 40s, female, Persian *
Kayván Sobhání	12, male, Persian-American *
Núrá (Sobhání) Golpaygání	28, female, Persian *
Rustam Golpaygání	30s, male, Persian *
(Parváneh Golpaygání)	infant, female – (a doll can be used)

* *The distinctions "Persian" and "Persian-American" refer to the character's basic cultural identification.*

** *The titles "Mr." and "Mrs. Sobhani" are used in the script to help clarify for English-readers who's who in the Sobhani household and not to suggest a special formality toward their characters.*

BAND OF GOLD

"And when He desired to manifest grace and beneficence to men, and to set the world in order, He revealed observances and created laws; among them He established the law of marriage, made it as a fortress for well-being and salvation, and enjoined it upon us in that which was sent down out of the heaven of sanctity in His Most Holy Book."

—Bahá'u'lláh

ACT I, Scene 1

The living room of Hal and Melinda Jennison. It is late afternoon and the room is dark. With what light there is, one can make out the clutter of a not-so-recent move-in: boxes, a ladder, drop cloths, plastic-covered furniture, newspapers, items retrieved from boxes, take-out food containers. A small work area has been carved out downstage with a reclining chair, some books and neatly stacked papers. Upstage center is the front door. Upstage right is the door to the kitchen. Stage right has two doors: one to a bedroom, the other leading off to a hallway. Stage left has three doors: the master bedroom downstage, the bathroom center, and another bedroom upstage. In the living room, there is a splendid hanging lamp[2], and tied to one side of it is a homemade banner reading "Welcome Home Africa Boy." We hear the clinking of keys at the front door. The struggle goes on longer than it should before the door finally opens. HAL *and* MELINDA, *both in their 40s, enter.* MELINDA *has an allergy mask.*

MELINDA: You need to fix that– (*Reacting to the heat in the house.*) Oh God, out of the pan...!

---

[2] The play may be performed without an actual lamp. This is almost preferable as the imagination of the audience may create something more magnificent than could be actually hung.

HAL: (*Inspecting door.*) It is the realtor's job to fix this, not mine…

MELINDA: We live in Florida now, you have to keep the A/C on.

HAL: You know I hate—

MELINDA: Wait.

She flips a switch, and the downstage lamp is illumined. The effect is somewhat magical.

HAL: Ah.

MELINDA: It was all I needed to know this was the right spot.

HAL: Yeah. (*He turns the main lights on.*)

MELINDA: Too bad we can't stay.

HAL: Don't start.

MELINDA: I will not live in a community where I am scorned.

HAL: "Scorned"—she didn't agree with your opinion.

MELINDA: It's not an opinion, it's the truth!

HAL: (*Looking proudly at banner.*) I don't know why you don't like this banner.

MELINDA: He's not a boy any more, and you shouldn't hang it on our chandelier.

He rolls his eyes at the word "chandelier."

MELINDA: You know I feel sorry for her, she is a repressed female.

HAL: She's a lovely and elegant woman.

She eyes him.

HAL: Who is repressing her? Her husband is a saint.

MELINDA: There's something not right with them.

HAL: Look, Parvin didn't accept your interpretation of Baháʼí law, that's all—

MELINDA: She looked at me like I was a piece of garbage on the street. That is not Baháʼí behavior, Hal!

HAL: And backbiting is?

MELINDA: Don't judge me.

ACT 1, SCENE 1

HAL: I'm not, I'm reminding you.

MELINDA: If I can't talk to my husband, who can I talk to? Everywhere I go, I run into people so steeped in denial that they project onto others all their own negativity.

HAL: Moving here wasn't my idea!

MELINDA: We moved to be here for my son.

HAL: Chris was fine here his freshman and sophomore years.

MELINDA: Having him out of the country changed my feeling about that. And he's going to need our support if he's going to be this… artist.

HAL: For the record, I moved here to save our marriage.

MELINDA: I wasn't going to divorce you.

HAL: You said you'd leave.

MELINDA: I was pre-menstrual—one more day in South Dakota, my head was going in the oven.

HAL: That's what you said about staying with your mother while I unpacked that tractor trailer—

MELINDA: (*Referring to disarray.*) And a nice job you've done.

HAL: (*Continuing.*) — full of CRAP I would have preferred to set fire to. Now again you want to leave?

MELINDA: Hey I didn't create this. The way Chris talked about this Sobhani family, it sounded like the perfect place to move, but they don't seem very welcoming of me.

HAL: You'll get over it.

> HAL *has settled into his recliner chair and opened his 'writing' station.' It includes all the paraphernalia of his work: pencils, pads of paper, mini-recorder, a little sign that has a picture of Einstein saying 'genius at verk.'*

MELINDA: You don't care if my spiritual light is extinguished.

HAL: This move has set me back six months, easily, on my book.

MELINDA: And?

HAL: I ain't movin'.

> HAL *has removed his jewelry, including a watch and a wedding ring.*

MELINDA: Why are you taking off your wedding band?

HAL: I have a ritual when I write: I detach myself from everything.

MELINDA: Your wife included?

He doesn't answer.

MELINDA: Fine. (*She exits, begins slamming things offstage. She comes back.*) We moved to Palm Terrace to establish an LSA and that's what I'll do, but if this is how I'm treated, I'm not going to the meetings. And if they elect me secretary, I'm going to scalp someone!

HAL: (*Still working.*) May I assume you're pre-menstrual now?

She hurls a sponge at him. CHRIS *has entered, looking sleepy, from the upstage left bedroom. He is brown-skinned (biracial) and he sports a thin beard. His hair is fairly big and funky, and his body, now shedding sleep, is generally spry, active, ready to bound. He has towel and toilet bag in hand.*

MELINDA: Hi honey, sleep well?

CHRIS: What up. (*He exits into the bathroom.*)

HAL: Well, their family is crazy about Chris. You have that in common.

MELINDA: (*Low.*) Did you know he was out past 3:30 this morning? With a friend, I guess.

HAL: Their girl—the one that goes to UF...

MELINDA: Tahirih.

HAL: ...she was upset Chris didn't come today.

MELINDA: Did you see their little Kevin come up to me so bright-eyed? "Are you Chris's mom?" Makes me feel I've done something in this life. Everything else is just a train wreck. (*Exiting into kitchen.*)

HAL: (*Not paying too much attention.*) She's just so radiant...

MELINDA: (*Off.*) There's no food in this kitchen!

HAL: Hey, but she said "See you tonight" as we were leaving—is there another holy day activity?

MELINDA: God help us—(*Reentering.*) Oh no.

ACT 1, SCENE 1

The sound of a gasoline-powered leaf-blower has been getting louder.

MELINDA: (*At the window.*) I hate those leaf-blower things. He's terrorizing my impatiens, Hal—go tell him to stop.

HAL: Just let the man do his job.

MELINDA: Sure, let the wife suffer—You have no spine. That's why you don't teach.

HAL: Oh-ho-hooo, don't go down that road.

MELINDA: I teach!

HAL: Whatever.

MELINDA: Okay, maybe I'm not the most successful teacher in the world, maybe the world cannot hear a woman with a strong voice, but you know what? I am an administrator! And you know what we are best at?

HAL: (*Picking up his things.*) I'm not going to participate in this.

MELINDA: Consulting. We don't run out of the room if we don't agree with something someone says.

HAL: (*Embroiled.*) Yelling and screaming is not consultation; it's not what Bahá'u'lláh had in mind.

MELINDA: Oh, so you know what He had in mind? I suppose all your Persian friends told you, because they're so good at consulting! Everyone sits around and smiles and nods and they won't tell you in English what they're really feeling, but when you see them among themselves: jibber-jabber-jibber-jabber! (*She has come from the kitchen with a glass of lemon water and now halts at the front door.*) Look, we won't tell Chris about today. We'll let them have their relationship and keep an arm's length.

She puts on an allergy mask and walks out the door. HAL sighs, and tries to get back to his writing. The barely audible patter of little feet is heard from the ceiling. CHRIS enters, humming "Maria" from "West Side Story."

HAL: (*Gesturing.*) Wait.

They are both quiet a moment.

HAL: Did you hear that?

CHRIS: (*Sings.*) "The most beautiful sound I ever heard…"

HAL: Sounded like little feet.

CHRIS: "Maria, Maria, Maria." Mind if I put my easel over here by the window?

HAL: Just move the boxes over there... (*indicating a pile.*)

CHRIS: Go siame, rra. (*Pronounced 'ho see-yah-me'.*)

HAL: Come again.

CHRIS: (*Clearing an area.*) That's Setswana for "just okay."

HAL: Ah.

CHRIS: (*Singing.*) "All the beautiful sounds of the world in a single word."

HAL: So I hear you were out til 3:30 this morning?

CHRIS: Guilty.

HAL: College buddy?

CHRIS: (*Singing.*) "Maria, Maria, Maria"

HAL: And his name is Maria?

CHRIS: No, but I know no song with her name. (*Sings fully.*)

> 'Maria... I just met a girl named Maria,
> and suddenly that name will never be the same to me...'

HAL: So she's cute?

CHRIS: (*Stops short his clearing out the area for his easel.*) Cute? (*Thinks.*) She is the lightning on the horizon after a long hot dusty dry season.

HAL: So will we meet Miss Lightning?

CHRIS: No doubt—Hey, this clock says 6:15.

HAL: That's what I got.

CHRIS: Did we miss the party?

HAL: No, we went. Your mother thought you needed your sleep.

CHRIS: Ah ssshhh–oot.

MELINDA *enters, through the hallway SR.*

MELINDA: I just had a profound teaching encounter.

ACT 1, SCENE 1

CHRIS: (*Peeved.*) You didn't wake me up!

He stops himself from saying more and exits into his room, closing the door.

MELINDA: What was that?

HAL: He's disappointed he didn't go to the holy day. I told you we should wake him up.

MELINDA *crosses to Chris's door and knocks.*

MELINDA: Chris, honey? (*Opens the door.*) Sorry, I would've woken you, but–jeez. (*She closes the door.*) So he just starts praying and ignores me? Does he seem different to you?

HAL: Not much.

MELINDA: (*Takes a deep breath.*) Anyway, I was talking to the yard man.

HAL: You mean the plant-hating terrorist?

MELINDA: I brought him some lemon water—'Abdu'l-Bahá used to give gifts to people who gave him trouble, so I thought I'd do the same. Turns out he was very friendly to me, and I felt inspired to invite him to a devotional gathering.

CHRIS *has reentered.*

CHRIS: I have a new rule: I "consume every wayward thought with the flame of His loving mention." When I'm upset, whatever it is, I pray and give it up…

MELINDA: We didn't do anything to upset you.

HAL: So—what's our plan for dinner?

MELINDA: I thought we'd take Chris out.

HAL: (*Looking at his wallet*) Sure, anything you want… under $20.

MELINDA: You cheapskate! I'm only going to have a salad anyway.

CHRIS: (*On the phone, dialing.*) You know I invited the Sobhanis over.

MELINDA: What?

CHRIS: I would have told you earlier but then nobody woke me up. (*Into phone.*) Hello, Parvin? Alláh-u-abhá, this is Chris…

MELINDA: You can't just invite people over like that.

CHRIS: (*Into phone.*) They are fine, thank you.

MELINDA: If you're talking about me, I'm not fine.

CHRIS: (*Into phone.*) Is Tahirih there?

MELINDA: Hal?

CHRIS: (*Into phone.*) Just when she wakes up. You're still coming tonight, right?

MELINDA: He's invited them over.

CHRIS: (*Into phone.*) No, I insist.

MELINDA: He's insisting, Hal.

HAL: What do you want me to do?

CHRIS: (*Into phone.*) Wonderful—see you soon. (*He hangs up.*) What are you shouting for?

MELINDA: Chris, you don't go inviting people over without consulting.

CHRIS: No big deal—we move the boxes into another room.

MELINDA: It's not just that. Look, I know you're close to them but there are some real issues here.

CHRIS: What?

HAL: (*Mocking.*) "There are thum real issueth."

MELINDA: Shut up you. Now I don't know what's going on underneath it all, but it's coming out with the typical control issues …

HAL: (*Mocking again.*) "Typical control issueth."

MELINDA: I need your support here, not your mockery.

HAL: Fine, your mother got into a little tiff with Mrs. Sobhani this afternoon.

MELINDA: It wasn't a *tiff*.

CHRIS: About what?

MELINDA: It's not important.

HAL: Do Bahá'ís have to clip their nails every week?

CHRIS: Seriously?

MELINDA: I just told her that's not what Bahá'u'lláh says—we can grow our nails, we can paint them—what she believes is a myth.

HAL: You don't dispel a myth by humiliating the person.

MELINDA: I was loving and frank…

HAL: And loud.

MELINDA: …and she gets this look like I just threw up on her. So seeing them now would be quite uncomfortable.

CHRIS: Mom, this is your Bahá'í community.

MELINDA: Yeah, and we got red flags flying left and right. (*Exits into kitchen.*)

CHRIS: I guess things in Africa were a little more life and death, you know? But hey, you just got off on the wrong foot!

The phone rings.

MELINDA: What is this insistence?

CHRIS: (*Answers the phone.*) Hello? Hey, I thought you were napping.

MELINDA: If that's them, we need to postpone.

CHRIS: (*Exiting into his room.*) Hang on.

MELINDA: Where are you…?—Hal, am I not speaking English?

HAL: Working!

CHRIS *reenters, still on the phone, now holding a Bahá'í prayer book. He speaks clearly, ostensibly into the phone, but so* HAL *and, especially,* MELINDA *will hear.*

CHRIS: A quote from 'Abdu'l-Baha: "The dearest wish of this servant of Thy Threshold is to behold the friends of East and West in close embrace; to see all the members of human society gathered with love in a single great assemblage, even as individual drops of water collected in one mighty sea."

MELINDA: The Bahá'í writings are not a club we use to bludgeon others into submission!

CHRIS *has exited into his room, closing the door. A knock on the front door.*

MELINDA: Oh, what now?

HAL: Probably your leaf blower.

MELINDA: (*Looking through window.*) It's Chad.

HAL *gets up, after the moment's hesitation it takes for his conscience to engage.*

MELINDA: (*Low.*) Look, I know he's going through a rough time, but we don't have room right now.

HAL: What do you want me to do, not answer the door?

MELINDA: Just tell him to come back… I don't know, another day.

She exits into the kitchen, and HAL *goes and opens the door. A heavy-set, African-American young man* (CHAD) *stands there.*

HAL: Hey Chad, how are you doing?

CHAD: Okay. Is Chris here?

HAL: Uh, he's on the phone. Do you…?

CHAD: Your wife gave me his email. I've been looking forward to meeting him… seeing him.

HAL: Oh, come on in for a minute—

MELINDA: (*From kitchen.*) Hi Chad!

HAL: So yesterday was tough, huh?

CHAD *nods.*

HAL: Why don't you have a seat?

CHAD *sits.*

MELINDA: (*Off.*) Hal, can I see you a moment?

CHRIS *enters, still on the phone.* CHAD *stands.*

CHRIS: Just a second, T. (*To* CHAD.) You're Chadwick.

CHAD: Chris?

CHRIS: My brother. (*He gives* CHAD *a big hug.*)

MELINDA: (*Entering.*) Chris, what did you tell them?

CHRIS: Beautiful, don't move. (*He's gone again.*)

MELINDA: So Chad…

CHAD: He's very good looking.

Pause.

MELINDA: Would you like a glass of lemon water? (*She has exited again into the kitchen.*)

CHAD: No thank you. (*To* HAL.) Can I use your rest room?

HAL: Right through there.

CHAD *exits*.

MELINDA: (*Off.*) I live in Florida and still have to buy lemons! (*Entering.*) Chad, do you like fresh squeezed lemon?

HAL: He's in the rest room.

MELINDA: (*Knocks on Chris' door.*) Is Chris still on the phone? (*She tries the door but it's locked.*) What does that mean 'he's very good-looking'?

CHAD: (*Re-entering.*) Excuse me…

MELINDA: Finding everything?

CHAD: Where's the light switch?

HAL: It's on the inside next to the mirror. Just between us, the toilet wouldn't let an egg yolk go through without getting clogged. If you need to pinch one, you can use the one in our room.

CHAD: This should be fine. (*Exits.*)

MELINDA: That was an undignified thing to say.

HAL: I have to write that down: "Egg yolk."

MELINDA: Oh, yeah, like you're going to use that in your book.

HAL: I don't censor what I write down.

MELINDA: (*Exiting into kitchen.*) Is this a book of bathroom humor?

HAL: That's an idea, you gotta read something when you're in there.

MELINDA: (*Off.*) Don't make me vomit.

HAL: It could be a new genre: each chapter is three pages long, and there's extra paper at the back… just in case. (*He laughs to himself.*)

MELINDA: (*Bringing in several glasses and a pitcher of lemon water.*) Have some lemon water, dear. Look: Chris needs to understand we're not ready for them, and as for Chad here, I don't know how to judge his reaction to Chris—

CHAD: (*Reentering.*) All set.

MELINDA: —will be right out. (*Offering a glass to* CHAD.) So how do you like your lemon squeezed?

HAL *spits out a mouthful of water.*

MELINDA: Hal!

HAL: (*Coughing.*) Ah!

CHAD: I'm sorry?

MELINDA: Slobs like you is why we need plastic on the furniture! Here.

She hands CHAD *a glass of lemon water.*

CHAD: I can't. The doctor said no citrus.

CHRIS *has reentered, off the phone now, carrying a big duffel bag.*

CHRIS: What happened?

HAL: Your mother is keeping us entertained as usual.

MELINDA: So you told them?

CHRIS: (*Standing underneath the banner.*) "Africa boy!" (*Making up super hero music.*) Dun-duh-duh-duh-Dun-dun-DUUUNNN! We join Africa boy as he's digging through his magical Bush bag... Gifts for everybody!

MELINDA: Right now?

CHRIS: For Hal, the mask of the warrior! (*Pulls out an African mask.*)

HAL: Cool. (*To* MELINDA, *holding the mask up to his face.*) Is this sexy?

MELINDA: Knock it off.

CHRIS: Mom, this is for you. (*Hands her a dark wood statue of a female.*)

MELINDA: Oh...

CHRIS: I got it at Victoria Falls. (*He enacts the Falls.*) Whssshhhh!! Water everywhere you look, falling almost as fast as the Zimbabwe dollar.

MELINDA: Does she have a name?

CHRIS: I just called it 'the weighty one' after lugging it in my gear so long.

MELINDA: Thanks, Chris.

CHRIS: No mathatha, as we say: no problem.

CHAD: Is that like hakuna matata?

CHRIS: Exactly. (*He takes out a necklace made of polished beads.*) This necklace was made by a very special African brother who said the beads are special for healing.

He puts the necklace around CHAD*'s neck. Tears well up in* CHAD*'s eyes, and he goes again into the bathroom.*

CHRIS: I feel good, spreading the love.

MELINDA: Chris, you might want to rein that back some.

CHRIS: (*Pulling out a colorful African cloth.*) Look at this cloth.

MELINDA: (*Taking a corner.*) Oh, look at that, Hal.

HAL: Who's that for?

CHRIS: (*Taking it back.*) That's a surprise.

MELINDA: Okay, so back to business: the Sobhanis took a rain check?

CHRIS: No, they're coming.

MELINDA: No, they're not, because I'm not ready to have them.

CHRIS: Ready or not—Take a whiff of that!

He has pulled a zebra skin out of his bag and sticks it under MELINDA*'s nose.*

MELINDA: (*Recoiling.*) Oh!

CHRIS: That's my zebra, Zamfir!

MELINDA: I'm going to be sick.

CHRIS: A gift from an African chief—Whenever I would forget where I was, Zamfir was there. (*He breathes deep.*) Yaaaaaaaggggh, Africa! (*He laughs.*) You want to smell, Hal?

He throws his arm around HAL *and makes him smell it.* MELINDA *has exited.*

HAL: Bleah!

CHAD *reenters, wearing the necklace.*

CHRIS: (*To* CHAD.) I can see the healing emanations just pouring off—Hey, why don't you stay for dinner?

MELINDA: (*Off, boiling over.*) That's it... I hope everyone likes fish sticks!

CHAD: What's the metal? Is it gold?

CHRIS: No, the place this comes from, they don't have gold to work with.

MELINDA: (*Slamming cabinets.*) Breaded fish sticks and hush puppies! That's what we have to feed everyone.

CHRIS: Manna from heaven!

MELINDA: (*Reentering.*) Boy, they're PERSIAN!!

CHRIS: So?

MELINDA: They brought a six course meal today to the celebration. They took the cheap cookies that Hal brought and displayed them on silver trays!

HAL: At least I brought something.

CHRIS: That's their culture, and they gotta understand the culture of where they're living.

MELINDA: I don't want to be an object lesson in American lack of refinement! (*Exits again.*)

CHRIS: Mom, I'll order pizza, or Chinese!

MELINDA: (*Off.*) I don't have enough spoons!

CHRIS: Chad-bro, you like Chinese?

CHAD: Uh...

MELINDA: (*She pokes her head back in, holds some plastic utensils in her hand.*) See Mrs. Sobhani, it's a spoon, but with little teeth too, like a fork. They call it a SPORK! (*She hurls some at* CHRIS.) I won't hurt you, Chad—why don't you come give a hand?

CHAD *reluctantly follows her into the kitchen.*

CHRIS: She's spunky.

HAL: You could have given some warning.

CHRIS: I have a surprise coming. (*He winks.*)

MELINDA: (*Off.*) I don't hear any cleaning!

HAL: Melinda, I told you I need to do some work to stay on schedule.

MELINDA: (*Off.*) Your schedule is no longer a priority. This place needs to be emptied.

CHRIS: Mom, back off the man.

MELINDA: (*Off.*) You may not speak another word. You are responsible for our crisis.

CHRIS: Did you say crisis? "Africa Boy" to the rescue!

MELINDA: (*Slamming cabinets.*) I am not happy!

CHRIS: (*With superhero voice.*) Melinda, come in here!

MELINDA: (*Off.*) Don't call me that!

CHRIS: (*Still with superhero voice.*) ME-LIN-DAAAAA!

MELINDA: (*Off.*) I do not deserve this...

CHRIS: That's the great thing about God—He blows away our expectations, Pugghshheww!

MELINDA: We're not talking about God, we're talking about a boy who doesn't communicate well.

CHRIS: A man! Africa Man, spreading peace and love through the land! (*Pulling her into the room to hug her in front of everyone.*) Melinda, open your arms! Wider! Come on, Hal!

HAL: That's all right, Chris.

CHRIS: (*Mocking* MELINDA.) "Hal, I need your thupport right now"—I'm teaching your wife a lesson.

HAL *laughs and comes over to join the hug.*

CHRIS: You too, Chadwick! This is it, Melinda, the oneness of the human family!

MELINDA: I don't like it when you call me that.

CHRIS: (*Mocking.*) "I don't like it when you call me that."

CHAD *has come close. The hug absorbs him too.*

CHRIS: Repeat after me: "I will no longer be sorrowful and grieved."

ALL: "I will no longer be sorrowful and grieved."

CHRIS: "I will be a happy and joyful being."

ALL: "I will be a happy and joyful being."

CHRIS: Now bring on the feast!

He pushes everyone and breaks up the hug.

MELINDA: Sometimes it's just so painfully obvious you're mine.

She goes to hug him and he flies away.

CHRIS: (*Out the door.*) Africa-Man!

MELINDA: And there he goes… (*At the kitchen door.*) Okay, Chad will finish washing the carrots, celery and tomatoes. (*Retrieving a kitchen knife.*) Hal, get Chris back in here and take these boxes out of here.

HAL: Got it covered. Now please do whatever you need to do to feel ready.

MELINDA: (*Gesturing with knife.*) What I need to feel ready is to see some progress here.

HAL: Why don't you give me that?

MELINDA: Don't mess with a woman with a seven-inch knife.

CHRIS: (*Having reentered.*) Still working on that power thing, huh?

MELINDA: I'm not working on anything, this is the man with the problem.

HAL: Give me the knife.

MELINDA: Chop, chop.

CHRIS: (*Sitting down, chewing on celery.*) See, you folks gotta see the people in the bush. The power thing was worked out centuries ago.

MELINDA: Great, so help me with the math—we have Mr. and Mrs. Sobhani…

CHRIS: Tahirih.

MELINDA: That's seven, how about Kevin?

CHRIS: Yeah, maybe.

MELINDA: Eight.

CHRIS: Her sister's in town, but I'm guessing not.

MELINDA: Nine!

CHRIS: They won't all come.

MELINDA: Nine people means two fish sticks a piece, figure three or four hush puppies, a small handful of chopped veggies…

CHRIS: Do you have rice?

MELINDA: (*Upset.*) Got a box of Uncle Ben's—

CHRIS: Mom, no one's going to remember tonight for the food. I've got something up my sleeve.

MELINDA: (*Leaving.*) Please just finish. Hal, leave the Bahá'í books where I can get to them.

CHRIS: What are you upset about? Just let it go and be happy!

She has exited into her bedroom. HAL *and* CHRIS *stand silently.* CHAD *enters holding handfuls of celery, carrots and tomatoes.*

CHAD: Uh, these are washed, what should I do now?

HAL: I gotta open a window in here. (*He opens a window and breathes in the air.*)

CHRIS: What do we do, boss?

HAL: Uh… Maybe you can move that table over there.

He points to an area downstage. CHAD *puts the vegetables on the table and as he and* CHRIS *are moving it, some of them fall on the floor.*

HAL: (*Annoyed.*) You're dropping…

CHAD: Oh.

HAL: I'll get that. (*To* CHAD.) Why don't you take this box to the garage.

MELINDA: (*Off, sneezing.*) Achooo! (*And again-*) Achooo!!

HAL: Did someone just drive in?

MELINDA: (*Off, sneezing.*) Is there a window open?

HAL: It's shut!

He slams the window shut. CHRIS *opens the door for* CHAD *who goes out with a box.* MELINDA *enters.*

MELINDA: Okay, I have some boundaries that I need to lay down.

CHRIS: They're here.

HAL: Oh jeez.

CHRIS: They only live a few minutes away.

MELINDA: (*Exasperated.*) I am not done.

HAL: Chris, table.

MELINDA: Respect me!

She exits to her room. HAL *and* CHRIS *move the dining table so it's centered beneath the lamp. The sound of people approaching the front door. Though the door is still open a crack, the doorbell rings. Hal opens the door to find six people. They are* TAHIRIH, *a young woman in her early 20's, her mother* (PARVIN SOBHANI), *her father* (SIRUS SOBHANI), *her younger brother* (KAYVAN). *Trailing behind these four are Tahirih's older sister* (NURA), *her brother-in-law* (RUSTAM), *and their infant daughter, Parvaneh.*

HAL: Holy Mackerel! Hello everybody.

THE SOBHANIS: Hello, Alláh-u-abhá, etc.

CHRIS: Hey you! (*He gives* TAHIRIH *a big hug, while the others look on.*)

TAHIRIH: Easy boy—

CHRIS: (*Laughs.*) Welcome to you all!

HAL: Come on in, everybody.

TAHIRIH: Thank you.

CHRIS: Sirus and Parvin, hál-e-shomá?

MELINDA: (*Entering.*) Hello, every—Oh dear God…

CHRIS: You know my mother everyone.

TAHIRIH: Some of us do, hello Melinda.

MELINDA: Hi. Hello, Parvin.

MRS. SOBHANI *nods her head graciously, but with a certain aloofness.*

HAL: Please come in.

MR. SOBHANI: Thank you.

There is head nodding and hellos, but no one actually comes far into the room because of the clutter.

CHRIS: (*To Tahirih's young brother,* KAYVAN.) Kayvan, give me some skin.

KAYVAN: (*Beaming.*) Hey Chris.

TAHIRIH: Chris, you remember Nura?

CHRIS: Of course, we met last year— (*To baby.*) And who is this?

TAHIRIH: That's Parvaneh, my four-month-old niece.

CHRIS: She's beautiful! Is this your foot?

NURA: This is my husband, Rustam.

TAHIRIH *walks away.*

CHRIS: So you're the mystery man—

RUSTAM *nods, but his reaction and overall presence are uncertain.*

MELINDA: I apologize for the state of our house—

TAHIRIH: Hey, this place is just like our house.

MELINDA: I'm sorry to hear that.

TAHIRIH: I mean, the shape and everything, don't you think, Dad?

MR. SOBHANI: Yes, similar…

TAHIRIH: Did you know that when you bought it?

HAL: No.

MELINDA: Of course we wouldn't have the same house as you on purpose.

KAYVAN: That's ironic.

MELINDA: That is ironic, Kevin. But on the other hand it just shows, you know, sort of the underlying unity…

HAL: One planet, one floor plan please. Come see our backyard and my bed of dying impatiens.

Some laugh. HAL *is leading them off through the stage right hall.*

MELINDA: Aren't you clever, Hal? Always making me sound like some long-winded, wind-bag.

She is last to exit. CHRIS *has pulled* TAHIRIH *to the side so they are alone.*

TAHIRIH: What are you doing?

CHRIS: I just have to tell you something.

He has come up close, she holds him off.

TAHIRIH: They'll be back in a minute.

CHRIS: Last night—the sea, the air, the moon, the sand beneath our feet—it was pure magic.

TAHIRIH: Yeah?

CHRIS: Yeah.

TAHIRIH: I have to tell you something: you can't just pick me up like that in front of my family.

CHRIS: I have something for you!

He has retrieved the African cloth. TAHIRIH *takes it and puts it on like a Persian head scarf.*

TAHIRIH: Right back to Iran.

CHRIS: No, no, no—let me show you. (*Taking the cloth and wrapping it around her like an African dress.*) Hold this under your arm, okay and I'll wrap this around, hmm…

TAHIRIH: Careful. You need a permit for that, you know.

CHRIS: You smile—I'm the one suffering here.

TAHIRIH: You call this suffering?

CHRIS: I do. (*Stops wrapping, points to one of her rings.*) You've got that on the wrong finger.

TAHIRIH: It's silver—silver rings can go on my thumb.

CHRIS: Hey, I just came from the African bush.

TAHIRIH: Isn't that where diamonds come from?

CHRIS: You're sly.

TAHIRIH: Anyway, you said it's not the real thing.

ACT 1, SCENE 1

CHRIS: I said it's a stand-in until I can afford something more befitting.

TAHIRIH: Boy, if you want something, you have to go after it full on!

CHRIS: Didn't I tell you I loved you and I wanted you to be my wife in this world and in all the worlds of God?

TAHIRIH: I seem to remember that.

CHRIS: What did you feel then?

TAHIRIH: I dunno.

CHRIS: Was your heart pumping fast?

TAHIRIH: Maybe.

CHRIS: And did you have this little bit of sweat on your forehead here, like you do now?

Voices heard off.

TAHIRIH: Okay, cool off, Romeo.

CHRIS: You said 'full on,' no?

TAHIRIH *goes to break away from* CHRIS.

CHRIS: Let me finish wrapping here. So are we going through with this?

TAHIRIH: Not til I signal. I dropped a hint to my parents—My mother wasn't going to come.

CHRIS *turns to see* MELINDA *leading the others in.* TAHIRIH *quickly takes off the cloth, moves away from* CHRIS *and starts folding the cloth.*

CHRIS: (*To* MELINDA, *singing* "Something's Coming" *from* "West Side Story") "There's something due any day, you will know right away…"

MELINDA: (*To* TAHIRIH.) You missed the tour.

TAHIRIH: Next time.

CHRIS: (*Turning to* TAHIRIH.) You took it off!

KAYVAN: Smells good!

MR. SOBHANI: I agree!

HAL: *(To* CHRIS.*)* I found out what that noise was—There's a squirrel chewed his way into the rafters.

RUSTAM: Like I say, I lend you my gun.

MELINDA: No guns thank you!

HAL: He chews on the wrong wire and all our lovely things go up in flames.

TAHIRIH: You don't want that.

HAL: Not til after I get some decent insurance. Chris, help me with chairs—

MELINDA: *(To* TAHIRIH.*)* It's a lovely pattern, that cloth. Chris gave me this. *(She shows the statue.)*

TAHIRIH: That's beautiful.

MELINDA: Do you like it?

HAL: Folks, please seat yourself around the dining table.

> *They gather around the dining table, around which are brought an assortment of chairs. Over the following dialogue, they settle into assorted chairs.* MELINDA *pushes in a nice desk chair.*

MELINDA: Parvin, would you like to trade with me?

MRS. SOBHANI: Thank you, I am fine.

MELINDA: It's just my back is a little funny from moving. Again I apologize, we didn't expect guests.

RUSTAM: Maybe we should not have come.

CHRIS: Nonsense, we're together!

MELINDA: I hope you like fish sticks and hush puppies—in tiny portions.

CHRIS: Our fishes and loaves!

> CHAD *enters from the front door. He has been absent since the Sobhanis arrived.*

CHRIS: Hey, Chadwick, where'd you go to?

CHAD: Just uh—telling my grandma. *(Goes into the kitchen.)*

HAL: Chad's our neighbor. He'll be joining us for dinner.

NURA: Oh, great. Is Chad a Bahá'í?

CHRIS: Not officially, but he's very interested in spiritual things. Right, Chadwick?

RUSTAM: That's great, Chad's not a Bahá'í.

NURA *gives* RUSTAM *a look, which he refuses to acknowledge.* CHAD *has returned to his chore of cutting the vegetables with a knife.*

MR. SOBHANI: You know, the house is similar, but this is much newer.

HAL: We'll have to judge for ourselves. When are we invited, Parvin?

MRS. SOBHANI: Oh.

HAL: I'm looking forward to tasting your bademjun again.

CHRIS: I can just imagine one man in the bush walking into another's mud hut and saying, 'You know this is of a very similar design and construction to our hut…'

TAHIRIH: We are in the same sub-division.

MELINDA: We weren't sure we could afford to buy in Palm Terrace, but Hal is a pretty good haggler.

HAL: I don't haggle.

CHRIS: Definitely a haggler.

HAL: It's just a poker face.

MELINDA: Yes, this Bahá'í is proud of his poker face.

CHRIS: The Guardian was asked if it was okay for Bahá'ís to play poker—guess what he said.

MELINDA: Tell him, maybe he'll develop some shame.

HAL: I almost never play—and I've never read anything against it.

MRS. SOBHANI: (*To* TAHIRIH.) Ún chí-e? اون چیه؟
    [*Translation: What is that?*]

TAHIRIH: Poker? Qomár bází. پوکر؟ قمار بازی.
    [*Trans: A gambling game.*]

MELINDA: Tell him, Chris, before he has time to hide in his fox hole.

MRS. SOBHANI: Gambling not good.

Laughter.

CHRIS: Parvin-jan, Shoghi Effendi was asked if poker, the card game with no money so no gambling, is poker okay for Bahá'ís? He said, (*Gesturing with his hands.*) 'The Bahá'ís have time to play poker?"

Everyone laughs except Rustam.

RUSTAM: You know why he said that.

Everyone quiets down.

RUSTAM: He wants to steal all our fun away.

Pause.

MELINDA: I think my hush puppies are burning.

HAL: Let me help you. (*To* CHAD.) Oh… you might want to cut those a little bigger.

They both exit.

CHRIS: What do you mean by your comment, Rustam?

NURA: He means nothing, that's his way of making joke.

TAHIRIH: Real funny.

MRS. SOBHANI: Mídúní chí dorost karde?   میدونی چی درست کرده؟
[*Trans: Do you know what she's making?*]

TAHIRIH: Chris, what is it we're having?

CHRIS: Fish sticks and hush puppies.

MR. SOBHANI: Puppies? What if we try bite them and they bite back?

Everyone laughs.

KAYVAN: Yeah, or if they bark at us. (*He laughs.*)

NURA: No, Kayvan, they're hush puppies, so they are well-behaved.

Everyone laughs again.

MRS. SOBHANI: Chí tu-she?   چی توشه؟
   [*Trans: What's in it?*]

NURA: Tú chí? Hush puppies?   تو چی؟
   [*Trans: In what?*]

TAHIRIH: We want to know what's in a hush puppy.

MRS. SOBHANI: (*Embarassed.*) Ah! Tahirih-jan.

CHRIS: Corn meal? No dog I'm pretty sure.

MRS. SOBHANI: Of course, of course.

CHRIS: In Botswana, they eat corn meal, but they call it mealie-meal. It's like a fist-sized lump of over-cooked grits covered in chicken fat.

RUSTAM: That is better than starving.

CHAD: They have a lot of AIDS there, right?

CHRIS: (*Pensively.*) Yeah.

MELINDA and HAL *enter with the food on pans.*

MELINDA: This is just embarrassing, but it's all we have...

MR. SOBHANI: Everything is great. (*He claps his hands together.*) I'm ready to try a puppy.

Everyone laughs.

KAYVAN: Me too—Arf! Arf! (*He dangles out his tongue and whines.*)

MELINDA: Chad, you want to bring over the vegetables that you have.

CHAD: Sure. (*He does.*)

HAL: And there's ketchup here.

TAHIRIH: (*To* CHAD.) Did you make salsa?

HAL: That's just very finely chopped.

CHRIS: Chadwick, I truly appreciate your service for our dinner. You gave more attention to those vegetables than I did to my first two years of college.

TAHIRIH: Maybe you should get a real major.

CHRIS: Like what, pre-dental?

TAHIRIH: It's a real major!

RUSTAM: So you are an artist—when can we see your painting?

CHRIS: It's been a while since I finished anything.

KAYVAN: *(Putting ketchup on his plate.)* Hey Chris, look the puppy is bleeding. *(He starts to whine like a dog.)*

TAHIRIH: Ba<u>ch</u>che, sáket. بچه، ساکت.

[*Trans: Boy, be quiet.*]

Nura puts her napkin to her mouth as if she feels sick.

MELINDA: Nura, go ahead and take some before Hal finishes them off.

CHRIS: What do you do, Rustam?

RUSTAM: Computers, graphic design.

MR. SOBHANI: Rustam now works with me, my jewelry store.

RUSTAM: Just temporary.

A beat. CHRIS *looks over to* TAHIRIH, *but she shakes her head.*

TAHIRIH: Hey Dad, show Chris your wedding ring.

MR. SOBHANI *complies, but without taking off the ring.*

CHRIS: Very nice.

MR. SOBHANI: Some rings are precious because their gems—this is precious because its history. It was my great, great grandfather's.

CHRIS: Is that turquoise?

MR. SOBHANI: Yes. Turquoise they say was thrown to side of road by Abá Badí—you know Badí?

CHRIS: Sure.

MR. SOBHANI: His father tossed big bag of turquoise to go with empty hands to Shaykh Tabarsi with Mulla Husayn.

CHRIS: Wow.

HAL: So someone less detached came by, found the bag of turquoise and your great, great grandfather ended up with a piece.

MR. SOBHANI: That is the story. My grandfather gave it my father, my father gave it me.

CHAD: And it's gold?

MR. SOBHANI: You want to see? *(He shows the ring to* CHAD.*)*

TAHIRIH: Now that's a ring, huh Chris?

CHRIS: Yeah.

TAHIRIH: (*Teasing.*) You don't just find something like that in a store in an airport as you're walking by.

MR. SOBHANI: It is not so important. Maybe I sell it—fill my tank with gas.

TAHIRIH: Get out!

CHAD: I would buy it if I had the money.

TAHIRIH: He's teasing—he has to give it to Kayvan.

CHAD: (*To* NURA.) What about your ring?

NURA: My ring does not fit me any more.

RUSTAM: You know what does that mean, Chad? Maybe she's not the same woman I married.

NURA: Azíyat nakon. اذیت نکن.
 [Trans: Don't be fresh.]

RUSTAM: I swear, my wife was like this. (*Indicates 'skinny'.*)

MRS. SOBHANI: (*To* NURA.) Cherá nemírí bekhábún-í-sh? چرا نمیری بخوابونیش؟
 [Trans: Why don't you go put her (Parvaneh) down?]

NURA *gets up with the baby, but* MR. SOBHANI *takes her hand.*

MR. SOBHANI: We can resize the ring.

CHAD: How?

MR. SOBHANI: (*Indicating.*) You cut here, put torch, high heat here to melt, let cool... the ring is fit.

TAHIRIH: (*Having taken the baby.*) Melinda, is there somewhere we can put the baby to sleep?

MELINDA: Oh.

CHRIS: Use my room. Just to the left.

TAHIRIH *takes the baby out, followed by* NURA.

HAL: You came from L.A.?

RUSTAM: Tehr-Angeles, a few months now.

CHAD: Where's that?

RUSTAM: Los Angeles—

MR. SOBHANI: They say Tehran-geles, because too many Iranians are there.

NURA: (*Off.*) OH!!

Everyone turns to look. TAHIRIH *enters with the baby.*

TAHIRIH: Chris, there's a really bad smell in here—It's okay, Parvaneh.

CHRIS: (*Getting up.*) Oh, you must have met Zamfir!

NURA: (*At door.*) Toálet Koja-st?   توالت کجاست؟
[*Trans: Where is the bathroom?*]

TAHIRIH: (*Pointing.*) Unjá, poshte saret.   اونجا، پشته سرت.
[*Trans: There, behind you.*] It's okay, Parvaneh. (*Bouncing her.*) Just a stinky smell, just a stinky smell.

CHRIS: That's my zebra!

TAHIRIH: We thought it was a blanket.

MELINDA: Oh, I remember those days, with a new baby. Well, I have a teaching story I'd like to share. Today, I spoke to the man who was cleaning our yard, and I mentioned that we were Bahá'ís. He hadn't heard of it before, so I shared with him and I invited him to come to a devotional meeting, once we got the house ready.

During the following, NURA *enters, takes the baby from* TAHIRIH, *and exits.*

TAHIRIH: What's his name?

MELINDA: You know, at some level, when two souls are communicating, names are… just like labels. I mean, you're tasting the insides of someone, you don't need to be told about surface stuff.

CHRIS: Tasting the insides!

MELINDA: Oh shut up.

ACT 1, SCENE 1

CHAD: I think I see what you're saying. It's kind of like online, in the chat rooms, you know that label that people take online, it's not their real name. So, like mine is loverboyblue2.

TAHIRIH *laughs.* CHAD *looks over at her.*

CHAD: No, it is.

TAHIRIH: I'm sorry. I wasn't...

MR. SOBHANI: Bíshtar bokhor.   بیشتر بخور.

Báyad tashvíghesh koní.   باید تشویقش کنی.

[*Trans: Eat some more. You should encourage him.*]

CHAD: What did he say?

TAHIRIH: He said he likes the hush puppies.

CHRIS: Chadwick, what were you saying?

CHAD: Oh, I think I forgot where I was going.

TAHIRIH: Chat rooms.

CHAD: Right, I was just saying when you get online, all you really have to go on is like the words that people say. You just get like their name, even though it's not their real name –and then there's the words, just letters and words. You're in your room and it's dark, and quiet, and these words is all the connection you have to that person. They could be thousands of miles away, and it's just like this little life sign – words and letters coming up on your screen.

TAHIRIH: Sounds kind of lonely. I mean great at the same time— that's how you connected with Chris, right?

MR. SOBHANI: It's wonderful we have power to connect all the world.

VARIOUS: Yes. Here, here..., etc.

A beat. TAHIRIH *signals to* CHRIS, *but he's in the middle of chewing.* MELINDA *instead seizes the moment.*

MELINDA: I just want to take this moment to—clarify something. Parvin, we got into something this afternoon I don't think we really wanted to or...

CHRIS *coughs with surprise and exchanges a look with* TAHIRIH.

MELINDA: …it was just so unnecessary, and I said something to you and, well, you…

MRS. SOBHANI: (*To* TAHIRIH.) Ma'zerat khâhí míkone? Okay, it's okay. معذرت خاهی میکنه؟ [...]
[*Trans: Is she apologizing?*]

MELINDA: (*Moving over to a stack of boxes.*) Right, well what's good is that we have consultation and the Writings to turn to. And we've got the Kitab-i-Aqdas here, so Hal, which box is it?

HAL: This probably isn't the best time.

MELINDA: (*Looking in boxes.*) No, I really want to move past this… I think we both do.

MRS. SOBHANI: Chí shod? چی شد؟
[*Trans: What's going on?*]

NURA *has reentered, evidently having laid the baby to sleep.*

CHRIS: (*Coming up to her.*) Mom, what are you doing?

MELINDA: I don't know why we haven't unpacked these yet—they're our most valuable possessions.

MRS. SOBHANI: Dáre durúghesh-o sábet míkone? Chún man ketábam-o ávordam. داره دروغشو ثابت میکنه؟ چون من کتابمو آوردم.
[*Trans: Is she looking for proof for her lie? Because I brought my own book.*]

MRS. SOBHANI *pulls out her own book out of her handbag.* NURA *sees this and pushes it back in the handbag.*

NURA: Nakhayr. Mámán, bezár kenár—Tahirih. نخیر. مامان، بذار کنار - طاهره.
[*Trans: No. Mom, put it away.*]

MELINDA: (*Turning.*) What are you saying, Parvin?

TAHIRIH: (*Catching on.*) She's not—we were just talking. (*To mother.*) Emshab darbáre-ye ín níst. امشب درباره این نیست.

ACT 1, SCENE 1

[*Trans: This is not what tonight is about.*]

MRS. SOBHANI: (*Relenting.*) Man nemíkhám, valí agar ú ketábesh-o bíyáre, manam míyáram. من نمیخواهم، ولی اگر او کتابشو بیاره، منم میارم.

[*Trans: I don't want to, but if she brings a book, I'll bring my book too.*]

NURA: Velesh kon. ولش کن.

[*Trans: Leave it alone.*]

MELINDA: Okay, I don't know where we put it. It's just a mess—thanks, Hal.

CHRIS: So…

TAHIRIH *shakes her head at* CHRIS *saying the moment is not right.*

CHRIS: …Mom, how long did you hold the lawn guy hostage?

MELINDA: Oh, am I not allowed to teach the Faith now because I'm not running around Africa with a rotting zebra skin?

CHRIS: Okay, okay…

MELINDA: Aren't you hot? Take this thing off.

She tugs at his long shirt sleeves, and he pulls his arm away.

RUSTAM: 'Ajab khánevádeh-í. عجب خانوادهای.

[*Trans: Nice family.*]

MRS. SOBHANI: Ye dúne máhí-e dígeh bokhor, saye khodet-o bokon. یه دونه ماهی دیگه بخور،سعی خودتو بکن.

[*Trans: Eat another fish stick, make an effort.*]

CHAD: What did they say?

TAHIRIH: They said the fish is good.

CHAD: What language is that?

HAL: Farsi.

CHAD: What's that?

TAHIRIH: Persian.

CHAD: Oh, right. Like Baha-la-la.

Six people correct his pronunciation.

ENSEMBLE: Bahá'u'lláh.

CHAD: Wow, you all said that at the same time.

TAHIRIH *laughs.*

CHAD: I still don't think I can say it.

CHRIS: It'll come with time.

RUSTAM *gets up and walks out the front door without saying a word.*

MELINDA: (*Re-entering.*) Where is he going?

TAHIRIH *signals to* CHRIS, *but* CHAD *speaks first.*

CHAD: So how do you all know each other?

MELINDA: We're all Bahá'ís.

CHAD: Uh-huh.

HAL: The Sobhanis moved here from Iran—if I've got this right—a few years ago after waiting almost two years in Turkey for visas.

MR. SOBHANI: That's right.

TAHIRIH: Except I came earlier than the rest on a student visa. So everybody... Chris has an announcement.

CHRIS: (*Standing.*) Yes, well, two part story. First, I want you to think for a second: Throughout all the dispensations of the past, names have been very important.

MELINDA: Oh brother.

CHRIS: Please—when Jacob wrestled the Angel, God named him Israel. When Saul was struck blind by the vision of Christ, he became Paul. In our Faith, Ali Muhammad became the Bab. Muhammad Ali became Quddus.

CHAD: Actually, Cassius Clay became Muhammad Ali.

Everyone looks at CHAD.

CHAD: Really, I did a book report on that.

CHRIS: (*diverted, but not defeated.*) Cassius Clay became Muhammad Ali. Fátimih Zarrín-Táj became Qurratu'l-ayn became TA-HI-RIH!

ACT 1, SCENE 1

TAHIRIH: That's right.

MELINDA: What are you getting at, Chris?

CHRIS: What I'm getting at Chris is that "Chris" is no more. My name is "Semowa."

HAL: Semowa?

CHRIS: Semowa.

MELINDA: That's not a name, it's a country.

CHRIS: (*Spelling it out.*) Not S-A-M-O-A. It's S-E-M-O-W-A.

KAYVAN: That's cool, what does it mean?

CHRIS: Glad you should ask. Semowa is the Setswana word for "Spiritual."

MELINDA: What's wrong with 'Chris'? I should have some say in this.

KAYVAN: My cousin's name is "Rohan" -- that means spiritual too.

TAHIRIH: I think the name sounds Indian, like Native American.

CHRIS: It has a certain multi-racial appeal, I'll admit.

KAYVAN: Seminole Casino!

HAL: So when are we supposed to start calling you this?

CHRIS: It's kind of like the phone company with area codes. It starts off optional, both work, and then...

CHAD: (*Imitating a phone company recording.*) Boo-do-DWEEEE! We're sorry. The number you have dialed is no longer in service, please check the number and try again.

CHRIS *laughs and claps. Everyone else is just startled.*

CHRIS: Beautiful, Chad-bro. I couldn't have done better myself.

He gives CHAD *a high five. A pause.*

TAHIRIH: Well, I like it, and I'm proud of Semowa. We need Bahá'ís who will stand up and be different despite what people say.

MELINDA: Are you going to change your name too?

TAHIRIH: I believe I am.

NURA: What?

KAYVAN: Augh, I want to change my name too!

He gets a glance from MRS. SOBHANI.

KAYVAN: Okay.

MELINDA: Tahirih, you have a beautiful name already, don't pay attention to this doofus.

TAHIRIH: I'm not talking about my first name.

MELINDA: What? Why would you change your last name?

She moves over to hold CHRIS's *hand. Realizations appear, pop-corn like.* MELINDA *starts choking and coughing.* NURA's *tears start and she goes to hug* TAHIRIH. TAHIRIH's *parents look calm having had some warning. Only* KAYVAN *is still out of it.*

TAHIRIH: Surprise.

KAYVAN: What are you going to change it to?

TAHIRIH: Manteha.

KAYVAN: That's Chris's name—O my...! (*He jumps and hides behind his chair, sticks his head up...*) So wait, that makes Chris, my...

CHRIS: Brother.

KAYVAN: Whoa, that's... that's so cool, Chris—I mean, Semowa.

HAL: I got to give it to you: that was some ace up your sleeve.

MELINDA: I can't feel my legs.

TAHIRIH: We know it's a surprise, but we've been thinking about it for months.

CHRIS: It's a beautiful thing, the coming together of East and West. The Persian martyrs and the American pioneers, and now with an understanding found in the bosom of Mother Africa herself—like two great seas coming together in... one big salty soup! Our children will be a new race of men.

He raises his glass; others join, some hesitantly.

MELINDA: Ah, excuse me, I don't mean to pop anyone's balloons but there is the little issue of consent—as in you need the

ACT 1, SCENE 1

approval of all biological parents—before you go making any grand announcements!

TAHIRIH: Melinda, that's why we decided to announce it with you all here.

MELINDA: You mean you planned it this way? Chris?

CHRIS: Semowa.

TAHIRIH: And we have a special request: Not only would we like my parents' and Melinda's consent, we'd like yours as well, Hal, because you've been like a father to Chris.

HAL: You don't need to do that—that stupid door.

RUSTAM has been trying to open the front door, but the door knob is sticking. CHRIS *runs to open it.*

CHRIS: (*Opening door.*) Hal, it's not up for discussion. It's as if Bahá'u'lláh sealed the matter Himself.

RUSTAM: (*Entering, very happy.*) Boy, I love fresh air!

NURA: Rustam!

RUSTAM: What's happening?

NURA: Tahirih o Chris míkhán arosí konan.   طاهره و کریس میخوان عروسی کنن.

[*Trans: Tahirih and Chris want to get married.*]

RUSTAM*'s happy expression disappears behind an opaque semi-smile.* CHRIS *goes to shake hands with him, but* RUSTAM *turns away and walks right back out, slamming the door. A beat where* CHRIS *looks at* TAHIRIH, *who looks at* NURA, *who looks to her parents.*

MR. SOBHANI: Maybe he doesn't know to show his happiness.

Lights fade. End of Scene.

"[M]arriage is dependent upon the consent of both parties. Desiring to establish love, unity and harmony amidst Our servants, We have conditioned it, once the couple's wish is known, upon the permission of their parents, lest enmity and rancour should arise amongst them. And in this We have yet other purposes."

—Bahá'u'lláh

ACT I, Scene 2

The Sobhani home, afternoon. What we see is the same structure as the Jennison home, but with a different décor and atmosphere. Where there was chaos in the former, here there is control; fine furnishings instead of boxes and Walmart furniture. It is elegant and comfortable, but air-tight, and now immaculately prepared for visitors. TAHIRIH *is putting plastic wrap on food dishes that are getting, by turns, either too cool or too warm.* NURA *sits on the couch, staring at a Persian language program on TV. A commercial comes on and she mutes the sound.*

TAHIRIH: So?

NURA: Az man chí míkháhí? ازمن چی میخواهی؟
    [*Trans: What do you want from me?*]

TAHIRIH: I want to know what you plan to do. Obviously, his ruining your life hasn't been enough to make you change—

NURA: Hích-chí darbáre-ash هیچی درباره‌اش نمیدونی.
    nemídúní.
[*Trans: You don't know anything about it.*]
    MRS. SOBHANI *enters through the front door.*

MRS. SOBHANI: Nemídúnam cherá nemígzáre man mas'úl-e qazá básham. Sá'at-e panj goftí, doros-e? Mígan Ámríkáíhá hamíshe sar-e vaqt míyán. Be har hál, mohem níst, shoharesh gúshtesh ámáde níst, va bábát khaylí, khaylí dír karde.

نمیدونم چرا نمیگذاره من مسئول غذا باشم. ساعت پنج گفتی، درسته؟ میگن آمریکایها همیشه سر وقت میان. به هرحال، مهم نیست، شوهرش گوشتش آماده نیست، و بابات خیلی، خیلی دیر کرده.

[*Trans: I don't know why he won't let me take care of the food. You said five o'clock, right? I don't understand, I heard Americans live by the clock. I mean, it's just as well, her husband's meat is not ready, and your father is very, very late.*]

TAHIRIH: Americans are just as late as anyone else unless there's money involved. And Mommy-jún, we're going to speak English today, okay?

MRS. SOBHANI: I don't know why the food he don't let me do!

NURA: He thinks it is big American thing, to have barbecue.

MRS. SOBHANI: Good, but why first time try when guest come?!

TAHIRIH: He's just trying to show off. He knows he screwed up bad this time.

MRS. SOBHANI has exited. NURA turns the TV sound back on.

TAHIRIH: You can't just ignore this!

NURA: Sshh.

TAHIRIH grabs the remote and mutes the TV.

TAHIRIH: So what did he have to say about last night?

NURA: I didn't talk to him.

TAHIRIH: Why not?

NURA: He came in late, and slept on the couch.

TAHIRIH: What kind of marriage is this?

NURA: You think it's all happy love and everywhere is flowers. You wait...

Through the front door, RUSTAM *enters with a chef hat, a red apron and a barbecue fork.*

RUSTAM: The fire-pit is blazing! (*To* NURA, *as if tempting her.*) Come, join me.

NURA *ignores him.*

RUSTAM: (*To* TAHIRIH.) How about you?

TAHIRIH *ignores him.* RUSTAM *retrieves a dish of marinated chicken kebab.*

RUSTAM: Okay, ain't nobody but us chickens. (*He exits.*)

NURA: You cannot just leave your husband when you are in tough times. I have a baby now.

TAHIRIH: Now I love Parvaneh, but we told you don't have a baby until...

NURA: How long could I wait? I saw him looking other women, and on Internet websites.

TAHIRIH: So divorce him!

MRS. SOBHANI: (*At door.*) Cherá saresh   چرا سرش داد می‌کشی؟
dád míkeshí? Ún khodesh náráhat-e.   اون خودش ناراهته.

[*Trans: Why are you yelling at her? She already feels bad.*]

TAHIRIH: The point is not that she feels bad, it's that she's not willing to do something about it.

NURA *turns the TV back on.*

TAHIRIH: Why are these blinds closed? Let the sunlight in.

NURA: Nah, nah, I have headache.

TAHIRIH: I wonder why!

TAHIRIH *grabs the remote and turns off the TV, then takes out the batteries and stuffs them in her pocket.* MRS. SOBHANI *has entered with a book.*

MRS. SOBHANI: Tahirih-ján. طاهره جان

TAHIRIH: Baleh, Mámán. بله، مامان.
[*Trans: Yes, Mom.*]

MRS. SOBHANI: Mádar, begú مادر، بگو معنیش چیه.
maaníyesh chí-e.
[*Trans: Tell me what this means.*]

TAHIRIH: Is that a cookbook?

MRS. SOBHANI: Kitáb-i-Aqdas. (*Reading, struggling with pronunciation*—) "It hath been enjoined upon you to pare your nails, to bathe yourselves each week…" Each week.

TAHIRIH: Mámán, why are you bothering with that right now?

MRS. SOBHANI: Khob, behtar-e, خب، بهتره، منم از وقتم
manam az vaqtam bará-ye برای کار دیگه استفاده
kár-e-dígeh estefádeh konam. کنم.
[*Trans: Well, I might as well use the time to do something.*]

TAHIRIH: Mámán, khaylí fársí harf مامان، خیلی فارسی
mízaní. You have – to speak – English. حرف میزنی.
[*Trans: You're speaking Persian too much.*]

MRS. SOBHANI: They late. Your father late. Kebáb late! I ready, and you yell me I use time study English in book?

MRS. SOBHANI *clicks her tongue, leaves the book on the coffee table and goes to the kitchen.* TAHIRIH *laughs at this display;* NURA *doesn't.*

TAHIRIH: You're going to participate in the Assembly meeting, right?

This was directed at her mother, now off. No response.

TAHIRIH: She's so funny. (*To* NURA.) Look at you, look at how miserable you are.

NURA: You don't know what a hell I'm in—How can I leave him when I have no job, no money?

TAHIRIH: No one's charging you rent here.

NURA: He would never agree to leave. He would get so angry, I don't know what.

TAHIRIH: See how afraid you are. That right there shows bad this has become.

NURA: He never hits me.

TAHIRIH: He doesn't need to! He keeps guns in your closet.

NURA: That is for hunting.

TAHIRIH: Yeah, big hunter!

MR. SOBHANI: (*Entering by front door.*) Hello.

TAHIRIH: Alláh-u-abhá, Bábá. (*She kisses him.*)

MR. SOBHANI: Alláh-u-abhá, azíz-am.

TAHIRIH: Go get changed, they'll be here any minute.

> MRS. SOBHANI *has entered and taken the grocery bag her husband has brought. She exits back to the kitchen without greeting him.*

MR. SOBHANI: (*To* MRS. SOBHANI.)

> Che-te? Bús-am koja-st?   چه ته؟ بوسم کجاست؟
>
> [*Trans: What's wrong? Where's my kiss?*]

TAHIRIH: We're all speaking English today, Dad.

MR. SOBHANI: Okay. Where is my kiss? (*He goes into the kitchen.*)

NURA: You know Daddy believes in him, that he can change.

TAHIRIH: Well Daddy doesn't know everything, does he?

NURA: What does that mean?

TAHIRIH: It means you need to be honest and tell him you're afraid.

> MRS. SOBHANI *reenters from the kitchen, followed by* MR. SOBHANI.

MR. SOBHANI: Busy, busy—no help today, so no lunch! I am starving.

TAHIRIH: That's okay, you need to work on your tummy.

MRS. SOBHANI: Eh! 'Porú' be   اه! 'پرو' به

> englísí chí míshe?   انگلیسی چی میشه؟
>
> [*Trans: How do you say 'porú in English?*]

ACT 1, SCENE 2

NURA: Bossy.

MRS. SOBHANI: Maybe Persian man better for you. American don't like bossy girl.

MR. SOBHANI: She's right—my brother in Ecuador… (*He gestures "skinny" with his hands.*) Nura-ján, try this on. (*He hands her a gold ring.*)

NURA: (*Putting on the ring.*) O Bábá, thank you

MR. SOBHANI: See? No end of the world.

NURA: My fingers are just so puffy. (*She fiddles with the ring.*)

MR. SOBHANI: We are so happy to have you home. (*Hugs her.*) All will be better, all will be… (*Exits.*)

TAHIRIH: Why won't you talk to him?

NURA: Rustam is a good man, but he cannot get good job. He works hard at English—I think he is depressed. Sometimes he act like this, sometimes we are most important in world to him. I need just get back to myself.

TAHIRIH: Listen, I didn't want to tell you this, but evidently you need to hear it—

NURA: What?

TAHIRIH: I think your husband has his eye on me.

   A beat. NURA *doesn't say anything.*

TAHIRIH: The way he looks at me… flirts. More than once he's walked in on me when I was in the shower. I caught him looking through my underwear drawer.

NURA: No.

TAHIRIH: Think about the way he behaved last night. This isn't just about you any more, Nura.

NURA: Maybe he is qaíratí! [غیرتی]

TAHIRIH: This is more than qaíratí! He's not protective, he's jealous!

NURA: You are saying this just because you hate him. You always hated him ever since Turkey.

TAHIRIH: No, I just never trusted him.

NURA: Not every one can have perfect man like Chris!

TAHIRIH: I don't say he's perfect, but at least I can trust him…!

NURA: No, Tahirih, that is so so so so wrong.

TAHIRIH: (*Overlapping.*) …and he's not going to try and control everything I do!

MRS. SOBHANI: (*At door.*) Velesh kon!   !ولش کن

[*Trans: Leave her alone!*]

TAHIRIH: Mámán, this plan to bring them here to save their marriage is not working.

RUSTAM enters, again from the front door.

RUSTAM: I'm ready for more kebáb. What are we talking about?

TAHIRIH: Tell him, Nura.

A beat.

RUSTAM: Tell me what?

The baby is heard crying. NURA *sighs and goes into the UL bedroom.* MR. SOBHANI *enters.*

MR. SOBHANI: How is our barbecue?

RUSTAM: Hot.

MR. SOBHANI: Good! We keep barbecue hot and house cool.

He closes the front door, which RUSTAM *left open, and takes him aside.* TAHIRIH *has exited into the kitchen.*

MR. SOBHANI: What is this?

He has taken out a piece of paper, a print-out of a website. RUSTAM *smiles, as if he has been waiting for this.*

RUSTAM: You need something to catch the eye.

MR. SOBHANI: Yes, gold, silver, diamond… It is jewelry store.

RUSTAM: (*Low.*) It's a pawn shop.

MR. SOBHANI: We are Bahá'í jewelry store. No place for the nice girl in swim suit.

RUSTAM accepts this quietly. TAHIRIH *has entered with a dish of meat for kebab, but she leaves it on the table rather than handing it to* RUSTAM.

ACT 1, SCENE 2

MR. SOBHANI: (*Turning upbeat.*) Come tomorrow, we'll make very nice website.

RUSTAM *turns, picks up the dish, and pauses at the door before leaving.*

RUSTAM: Tahirih-ján, I want to say sorry for last night. I was surprise. Always, we thought you would marry a Persian man. More than anything, I want you to be happy.

TAHIRIH *doesn't acknowledge his apology.* NURA *has reentered with the baby.*

RUSTAM: Okay. (*He exits.*)

NURA: She doesn't like Persian men anymore.

TAHIRIH: That's not true, I love my father. (*She kisses her father.*)

MR. SOBHANI: Two kisses? I must be the lucky man.

NURA: Lucky man with big decision to make.

TAHIRIH: And what is that supposed to mean?

MR. SOBHANI: I'm going to get dressed.

He exits. NURA s*hakes her head at* TAHIRIH.

TAHIRIH: Don't shake your head at me—you think I'm being nice to Bábá because of consent? You're the one who cried and cried until they gave in, now you still cry and cry…

MRS. SOBHANI: Tahirih!

TAHIRIH: I didn't start it.

MRS. SOBHANI: Hích qolí nemídím ke áreh yá nah.

هیچ قولی نمیدیم که
آره یا نه.

[*Trans: No guarantees! We decide yes or no.*]

TAHIRIH: I'm not saying you don't decide.

Doorbell.

TAHIRIH: It's them.

NURA *runs to her room.* TAHIRIH *opens the door.* CHRIS *enters, then* HAL *and* CHAD, *then a glum* MELINDA. *Assorted greetings.*

CHRIS: (*Giving* TAHIRIH *a hug.*) Hey T!

TAHIRIH: (*Resisting hug.*) Hey.

CHRIS: You okay?

TAHIRIH: Fine—Hello Hal, hello Melinda—welcome.

HAL: Hey Tahirih.

MELINDA: Hi.

> MRS. SOBHANI *is now there to greet her guests.*

TAHIRIH: Hi Chad, we're happy you could come. (*To* CHRIS.) Did you get held up?

HAL: Sorry, we figured Persians say five, they mean five-thirty or six, right?

MRS. SOBHANI: Please come.

CHRIS: Hey, do you mind if I bring in a painting I want to show?

TAHIRIH: Okay. Please have a seat, Melinda, Hal...

HAL: This place is a lot like ours.

> MELINDA *seems uncomfortable and resists being ushered to a seat, choosing instead to look around. This has its effect on* HAL *and* CHAD *as well.* CHRIS *reenters with a painting canvas, covered with a cloth, and a simple easel. He places the canvas on the easel downstage with the painting, still covered, facing upstage*

CHRIS: Looks like we got some fire out there!

HAL: Yeah, your neighbor's got his jockeys all in a knot.

TAHIRIH: What?

HAL: It's an old guy, he's out there with his hose watering the edge of his property.

TAHIRIH: (*Suppressing irritation.*) Really?

MRS. SOBHANI: Cherá nemígí beshínan? چرا نمیگی بشینن؟

> [*Trans: Why don't you ask them to sit?*]

TAHIRIH: Dáram sa'íy mikonam. دارم سعی میکنم.

> [*Trans: I'm trying.*]

CHRIS: (*Checking out the food.*) Smells great... like tadíg.

HAL: What, no hush puppies?

ACT 1, SCENE 2

This is a playful jab at MELINDA, *trying to rouse her. She mimics him darkly.*

HAL: Just a joke, dear—

TAHIRIH: The food is all ready, except the kebab.

HAL: (*Going back out.*) —maybe I'll go see what the cook's up to.

TAHIRIH: Oh. Maybe the rest of us can sit. My Dad should be right out.

    TAHIRIH, CHRIS, *and* CHAD *sit while* MELINDA *hovers.*

CHRIS: Mom, you want to sit?

    She doesn't respond. MRS. SOBHANI *enters with a tray of cold drinks.*

CHRIS: What—no tea?

MRS. SOBHANI: You want tea?

TAHIRIH: Boro, dígeh, he's just joking.   برو، دیگه [...]

    [*Trans: Don't worry...*]

    MRS. SOBHANI *exits.*

TAHIRIH: (*To* CHRIS.) It's so hot, why are you wearing long sleeves again?

    KAYVAN *runs in, wearing a hat.*

KAYVAN: Semowa, guess what I did today!

    He pulls off his hat to reveal hair teased up and braided to look like Chris's.

CHRIS: Ho-ho! Kayvan, you be stylin'!

MELINDA: Wow, Kevin, your hair kind of looks like Chris's.

CHAD: Who did that?

TAHIRIH: I did.

CHAD: Do you want to be a hair stylist?

MRS. SOBHANI: (*Seeing his hair for the first time.*) Bachche!   بچه!

    [*Trans: Child!*]

KAYVAN: I'm black now!

MRS. SOBHANI: Tahirih, che kár kardí?   طاهره، چه کار کردی؟

    [*Trans: What have you done?*]

CHRIS: Yeah, you got some black–

TAHIRIH: Khaylí dústesh dáre, míkhád mesl-e-ún báshe.   خیلی دوستش داره، میخواهد مثل اون باشه.

[*Trans: He adores him and wants to look like him.*]

MRS. SOBHANI: Qíyáfe-ash ayn-e meímún-e. (*Returns to kitchen.*)   قیافه‌اش عین میمونه.

[*Trans: He looks like a monkey.*]

TAHIRIH: Englísí harf bezan.   انگلیسی حرف بزن.

[*Trans: Speak English.*]

CHAD: What did she say?

TAHIRIH: I was trying to get her to speak English. What did you ask me before?

CHAD: Oh, if you wanted to be a hair stylist.

TAHIRIH: God no, a dentist. (*To* KAYVAN.) Boy, let me fix this—you've messed it up already.

CHRIS: Your mother is a hair stylist, isn't she, Chadwick?

CHAD: She's a specialist in African weaves and braids. She lives in Plant City.

CHRIS: (*Playfully getting in her face*) Maybe your mother could teach Tahirih how to deal with nappy-headed chillens.

TAHIRIH: I'm sure.

KAYVAN: (*To* TAHIRIH.) Ow, you're hurting me.

   HAL *and* RUSTAM *enter.*

HAL: (*To* RUSTAM.) Most times, things take more time than we expect. So this is a major point of my book: concentrate on what you can do best and leave the rest. Take as much time as you need.

RUSTAM: But time is money.

HAL: Time is abundant. We really have all the time in the world.

CHRIS: That's how you feel in Africa. Hey, I want to show everyone my painting.

ACT 1, SCENE 2

RUSTAM: I have something to show you, Africa. (*He exits into his room.*)

HAL: In Africa, you didn't have all the time suckers around—things that get in the way of what you need to do.

MELINDA: I assume you're not speaking of me.

HAL: (*Dodging.*) Mostly, things we haven't yet learned to take in moderation: TV, the Internet, cell phones… things that add to this general anxiety that I call "The Burden of the Undone."

MELINDA: No offense, honey, but you're bordering on being a time sucker yourself.

   HAL *fumes up.*

MELINDA: Just a little joke, dear.

CHRIS: (*With sarcasm.*) Nice.

   RUSTAM *reenters with a rifle, which he raises and points at* CHRIS.

CHRIS: Ho, ho, ho!

TAHIRIH: Rustam!

RUSTAM: (*To* CHRIS.) Keep your pants on, you will be fine. (*Puts up the gun, to* HAL.) Twenty-two caliber: good for squirrels in attics.

HAL: (*Taking gun.*) Oh, great, thanks.

RUSTAM: My gun for people is bigger. (*He slaps* CHRIS *on the back and exits.*)

MELINDA: That was different.

CHRIS: Okay, so what's the deal here?

TAHIRIH: That's it. (*She gets up and exits into Nura's room.*)

KAYVAN: (*With basketball. To* CHRIS.) Can we play?

CHRIS: In just a minute.

HAL: (*With gun, imitating Yosemite Sam.*) Say your prayers, varmint.

MELINDA: Put that thing down!

MR. SOBHANI: (*Entering.*) Alláh-u-abhá, everyone.

   Greetings are exchanged. NURA *enters with* TAHIRIH.

NURA: *(To* TAHIRIH.) Míkháhi che kár ‎میخواهی چه کار کنم؟‎ konam? —Chris, I am sorry, my husband has bad sense of humor.

[*Trans: What do you want me to do?*]

CHRIS: It's okay, it's gone. I would like though to share my painting with all of you.

People gather around.

CHRIS: I was up till five working on it. I call it "The Dawning of Love."

He reveals it. There are expressions of initial surprise. Time passes while everybody soaks in the painting, waiting for the next person to comment.

MR. SOBHANI: It's red!

CHRIS: *(Nodding.)* Yeah.

The silence deepens.

NURA: *(Pointing to one area.)* I like this.

MR. SOBHANI: Mm-hmm.

Others agree and nod.

CHRIS: See, that's the genesis, where Love is born—God's love for His own entity.

MELINDA: I don't know that I would have got all that from a squiggle and a dot.

CHRIS: *(Bristling.)* Well, there are the four kinds of love that 'Abdu'l-Bahá talks about, and there's the edgy, angry side of love like… with Rustam.

NURA: I see.

CHRIS: Bahá'u'lláh says all the red in the world is from Love, or an expression of Love, something like that. There are some references to other abstract expressionists…

People start to drop away.

MELINDA: Thanks for sharing, Chris—speaking of art: Tahirih, are you interested in a switch? *(Pulls African statue out of her Kenya bag.)*

ACT 1, SCENE 2

TAHIRIH: What do you mean?

MELINDA: I sensed that you didn't really get off on the Africa cloth.

CHRIS: Mom, what are you doing?

MELINDA: Making a trade—

CHRIS: Hey, I chose those gifts with care.

TAHIRIH: It's okay—(*Going to take the statue.*) Here Melinda.

CHRIS: (*Trying to make light of it.*) Look, I lugged that statue across Zimbabwe for you.

MELINDA: Yeah, and now every time I look at it that's what I remember.

MR. SOBHANI: So everybody, we're going to have our first Assembly meeting?

TAHIRIH: We should have just enough time to eat and clean up.

MELINDA: When will the food be ready?

HAL: He said ten minutes.

CHRIS: Great! Maybe we could take this time to consult.

HAL: About what?

CHRIS: Oh… about a certain marriage and whether or not it should happen.

TAHIRIH: Oh.

MELINDA: That's completely inappropriate.

CHRIS: Just opening up a conversation with you four. The rest of us will go shoot hoops.

MRS. SOBHANI: (*To* TAHIRIH.) Nemíkhám khodesh-o kasíf kone. نمیخواهم خودشو کثیف کنه.

[*Trans: I don't want him getting dirty.*]

TAHIRIH: I'll watch him.

CHRIS: See you soon.

MELINDA: (*To* CHRIS.) Hey, who said giving consent was a group activity?

They are out the door. Only the parents remain.

MELINDA: This isn't awkward.

HAL: It's as good a time as any—Is anyone so gung-ho that they're ready to toss in their chip?

    MRS. SOBHANI *laughs and nods her head.*

HAL: Parvin?

MRS. SOBHANI: Yes, yes.

HAL: You're ready to say yes?

MRS. SOBHANI: Sorry?

MR. SOBHANI: Míporse áyá ámáde-í   می‌پرسه آیا آماده‌ای که

    ke resáyat bedí.   رضایت بدی.

    [*Trans: He asked if you are ready to give consent.*]

MRS. SOBHANI: Oh, sorry, sorry.

HAL: I guess not.

    CHRIS *enters carrying a woven bag with an African pattern.*

CHRIS: Sorry... Something that might help you along. (*He pulls from the bag a wooden bowl and 4 stones.*) This is the consent bowl. Each of you gets a stone. (*He hands out the stones ritualistically.*)

MR. SOBHANI: What's this for?

CHRIS: This stone represents the responsibility God has placed on you and for which you will be held accountable.

MELINDA: Why are you looking at me?

CHRIS: You take the stone and when your heart whispers to your conscience the way dawn whispers its approach to the birds and it tells you that Tahirih and I should be bound together throughout all the worlds of God you place the stone in the bowl as a gesture of your consent. Once there it represents your life-long commitment to ensuring the unity and successful integration of our two families.

MRS. SOBHANI: (*Looking at her stone.*) From Africa?

CHRIS: Could be. (*He exits.*)

ACT 1, SCENE 2

MELINDA: (*Mocking.*) "Just starting the conversation."

MR. SOBHANI: Your son speaks very well. I like him very much.

MELINDA: Enough to give him your daughter?

MR. SOBHANI: (*Laughing.*) Yes yes, that is the question.

MELINDA: Look, I know the idea of an American son-in-law is enough to scare the pants off your typical Persian parents, let alone a black one –

HAL: Melinda…

MELINDA: It's true. All these Persians, even when they're born here, they still marry other Persians.

HAL: Yes, and whites with whites, blacks with blacks.

MELINDA: Right, and I'm not saying this because I'm Chris's mother, but he is a really special young man.

MR. SOBHANI: You are ready to give consent?

MELINDA: Heck no!

RUSTAM: (*Entering.*) Hello! They told me not to disturb you.

He walks into the kitchen and starts searching for something, slamming cabinets and drawers.

MELINDA: How's the fire?

RUSTAM: Great, I ask Chadwick if he brought an animal for sacrifice. I told him that Bahá'ís have rituals too, and one of them is sacrifice animals. He turned white as Hal! (*He laughs.*)

MELINDA: Well, he's very gullible.

RUSTAM: Let us say trusting. We Bahá'ís don't want to backbite.

MELINDA: I didn't mean it that way.

RUSTAM: Of course. (*He comes back in with a cup full of ice and a basting brush.*) So, marriage is great, yes? All we wanted was to peek beneath the sheets and—slam!—chains and heavy weights on your arms and legs.

RUSTAM laughs and exits, chewing on ice.

MELINDA: He's an odd one.

MRS. SOBHANI *gives* MR. SOBHANI *a look.*

MR. SOBHANI: So, no marriage is guarantee. The question—like your poker—do we see good gamble?

HAL: Sorry, I feel out of place.

MELINDA: The boy said he wanted you here.

HAL: Bahá'u'lláh didn't say He wanted me here.

MELINDA: Bahá'u'lláh may have changed the rules if He knew the details. (*Seeing open book on coffee table.*) Here's the Kitáb-i-Aqdas—I was looking for this last night!

A beat in which MELINDA *and* MRS. SOBHANI *exchange a look.*

MELINDA: But I guess that can wait.

MRS. SOBHANI*'s posture eases some.*

HAL: (*Tossing his stone in the air.*) For starters, maybe we can go around and everyone can give a yes, no, maybe so…

MELINDA: I think they're out of their minds. My son is.

MR. SOBHANI: He's in love. In Seven Valleys, Bahá'u'lláh says the love burns to nothing, to ash, all what reason has grown.

MELINDA: What about her? She doesn't seem so in love.

MRS. SOBHANI: (*Disagreeing.*) Uh…

MELINDA: What?

MRS. SOBHANI: (*To* HAL.) Tahirih now, she walk around… (*She makes funny eyes and waves her hands mimicking her daughter.*) She always tell family what do, what not do.

MELINDA: So that's different for her?

MRS. SOBHANI: I see different.

MR. SOBHANI: We should show you phone bills.

MELINDA: But where did this come from? The boy never tells me anything.

MRS. SOBHANI: The last summer—Bahá'í club—they do activity for children.

MELINDA: So were they dating then?

ACT 1, SCENE 2

MR. SOBHANI: To be honest, I think Tahirih was not much interested.

MRS. SOBHANI *waves her head back and forth indicating she's not so sure.*

MR. SOBHANI: But email—Chris begin sending long emails that changed. She read them out loud.

MRS. SOBHANI: "Oooh, Chris do this." "Mmm, Chris say this."

MELINDA: How are they going to live, by selling his art? Sorry, I've got to cover this up. (*Goes to cover painting with cloth.*)

KAYVAN: (*Entering, jubilant.*) Bábá! Bábá!

MELINDA: Slow down, sport.

KAYVAN: Semowa was all the way across the street and threw it and whoosh –it was awesome! Maybe he could move in with us, and I was thinking, um, um, that would just be… (*deep breath*) really cool. Oh, I forgot.

He runs out leaving the door open. Dribbling is heard.

MR. SOBHANI: He has consent of Kayvan.

MRS. SOBHANI: (*To husband.*) Páshím   پاشیم بریم

berím tú-ye ún otáq.   توی اون اطاق.

[*Trans: Let's go into the other room.*]

MR. SOBHANI: Melinda and Hal, perhaps we have privacy if we go to the other room.

They exit through UR door, leaving the bowl and stones behind. CHRIS *enters with the basketball, which he turns and passes back out the door.*

CHRIS: Think quick!

CHAD: Ow. (*He enters rubbing his chin.*)

CHRIS: Oooh, sorry there, Chad-bro! (*He throws his arm around* CHAD *and laughs.*) Ooh, you sweaty! T.O. while I do the P.O. (*He heads for the bathroom.*)

Now alone, CHAD *pulls from his bag a hand-held recorder, and begins to speak.*

CHAD: April twenty-second, 3:50 pm. Home of... people from Iran. Hit in the chin with basketball—Also, dry mouth, fatigue. Still the hair is the main thing I'm thinking about.

CHAD *is now by the couch, looking at his reflection in the coffee table. He spots the Kitáb-i-Aqdas open on the coffee table. He is not sure if it's okay to touch it.*

CHAD: (*Again speaking into the recorder.*) Looks like one of their books... (*Looks at cover.*) "The Most Holy Book." And it's right on the table, open. I can't imagine what words might be found in such a book.

As he's about to read, KAYVAN *throws open the front door.*

KAYVAN: Mom, he wants the vegetables now! (*Turns and calls.*) She's not here!

He goes back out. TAHIRIH *enters and heads for the kitchen.*

TAHIRIH: How are you doing, Chad?

CHAD *freezes.* TAHIRIH *comes out with a tray of vegetables and exits.* CHAD *again speaks into his recorder.*

CHAD: I closed the book on accident. I'm going to open it to a random page, and point to a sentence and read. (*He does this.*) Page 39, middle of the page. "Cast away that which ye possess, and, on the wings of detachment, soar beyond all created things." (*Touched.*) "Cast away that which ye possess." That easy?

MR. SOBHANI *enters.* CHAD, *slightly embarrassed, turns off his recorder and leans forward as if to hide what he is doing.*

MR. SOBHANI: Ah, Most Holy Book. You go straight to the heart, yes?

MR. SOBHANI *pats him on the shoulder.* CHRIS *enters from the bathroom.*

MR. SOBHANI: He's the man I am just looking for.

CHRIS: Me?

MR. SOBHANI *ushers* CHRIS *through the UR door. After a beat of quiet,* CHAD *starts back with the book and the recorder.*

ACT 1, SCENE 2

CHAD: "Know ye from what heights your Lord, the All-Glorious, is calling?" (*He stands up, paces a bit with closed eyes, and begins to do a spoken word improvisation.*) Calling, calling. Do you know from what heights He's calling, calling? Lord All-Glorious is calling, calling. Lord calling.

The phone rings. CHAD *turns and looks at the phone, dropping the book and the recorder, walks towards the phone. When he's just about to pick it up,* NURA *rushes in and grabs it.*

NURA: Allo. Alláh-u-abhá! Thank you, Chad.

She rushes back to her room with the phone, speaking Persian. CHAD *puts his hand to his heart as if it's beating fast.* TAHIRIH *enters again.*

TAHIRIH: He's going to set that tree on fire. (*To* CHAD.) Where's Chris?

CHAD *points to the UR door and picks up the book and the recorder.*

TAHIRIH: Do you know why?

CHAD *shrugs.*

TAHIRIH: Are you nervous or something?

CHAD *rises and walks to the bathroom.*

TAHIRIH: Okay, he's not friendly.

CHRIS *and* MR. SOBHANI *are at UR door.*

CHRIS: I don't know. Maybe 150, 200…

MR. SOBHANI: Let me know. (*Exits.*)

TAHIRIH: Hey.

CHRIS: Your dad just offered to help sell my painting in his store.

TAHIRIH: What he should do is hire you and get rid of Rustam.

CHRIS: I couldn't do that anyway, I want to paint this summer.

TAHIRIH: You okay?

CHRIS: Just my mother, she was giving me the eye… I've got to say a prayer.

TAHIRIH: Hey, why did you make such a big deal about the statue?

CHRIS: I can't let her get away with that.

TAHIRIH: If my future mother-in-law and I make a trade, that's good, no?

CHAD reenters. TAHIRIH *stops talking.*

CHRIS: How you doing, Chad?

CHAD: Okay. (*He goes out the front door.*)

TAHIRIH: What's wrong with him?

CHRIS: What do you mean?

TAHIRIH: He looks at me like I'm trying to steal you away.

CHRIS: Don't be silly.

TAHIRIH: Tell me, Chris, why is that no one takes my point of view seriously?

CHRIS: Okay, I don't know where this is coming from, but look: Chad's sick.

TAHIRIH: Don't tell me he has AIDS.

CHRIS: What if he did?

TAHIRIH: Don't look at me like I'm insensitive.

CHRIS: He doesn't have AIDS.

TAHIRIH: I don't want anyone to have AIDS.

The front door opens. It's CHAD *again, and again* TAHIRIH *stops talking.*

CHAD: Too hot. (*He looks at them a moment.*)

CHRIS: (*To* TAHIRIH.) Are you okay?

TAHIRIH: (*Annoyed.*) I'm fine.

CHRIS: Okay, time for a group hug—Chad, come here! (*He pulls the other two together.*)

TAHIRIH: (*Resisting.*) Don't push, okay?

CHAD: C'mon, girlie... (*He tugs on the back of her hair playfully.*)

TAHIRIH: Hey, you pull my hair, I'm going to pull yours!

She turns around and impulsively grabs the back of his hair. A clump of it comes out in her hand. He screams. She screams.

CHAD: Aaaaahhhhh!!!

ACT 1, SCENE 2

TAHIRIH: AAAHHHH! O my God!

CHRIS: Ho now!

CHRIS takes a flying leap away. CHAD stops screaming and starts to laugh.

TAHIRIH: Why are you laughing?

The UR door opens and the parents are there. CHAD *laughs louder.*

TAHIRIH: Stop laughing, I pulled out your hair!

CHAD: (*In a silly voice.*) And I pulled a funny on you.

TAHIRIH: What?

MELINDA: What happened?

CHRIS, amazed, tries to speak gently and without laughing.

CHRIS: It's nothing everyone, just go on back to your deliberations…

They do, with some exasperated expressions.

TAHIRIH: I'm waiting—

CHRIS: Honey—the reason his hair came out is that he has cancer and has started chemo.

CHAD: That be da bes' explication of the sich-a-ation.

TAHIRIH: Did you plan this?

CHRIS: No, I swear!

TAHIRIH: That is sick. (*She throws the clump of hair at* CHRIS.)

CHRIS: Look, T, it was just really funny to see you…

KAYVAN *bursts in the front door.*

KAYVAN: Our neighbor's calling the cops!

TAHIRIH: What?

KAYVAN: On Rustam.

TAHIRIH: Get Nura out here. (*At the door.*) You'd better grow up, Semowa.

She exits, going outside. CHRIS *sighs.* CHAD *picks up the clump of his hair.* KAYVAN *has gone into Nura's bedroom.* NURA *comes rushing out.*

NURA: (*At the door.*) Rustam! Leave that man alone! (*To* KAYVAN.) Stay there. (*Heading off.*) Mr. Nelson...

She runs out. CHAD, CHRIS *and* KAYVAN *go to the door to look.* CHAD *has sobered some, and tries to catch a reflection of his hair.*

CHRIS: That was hysterical—I don't know why she got so upset.

CHAD: Can you tell?

CHRIS: Not really.

RUSTAM *enters, and* NURA *behind him.*

NURA: Go in there and calm down.

KAYVAN: Are the cops coming?

NURA: Tahirih is talking to him.

RUSTAM: If I want to set my tree on fire, that is my business! Not the little raisin man next door.

NURA: This is a Bahá'í home. Chris, come.

She and CHRIS *exit.* KAYVAN *runs after them.* CHAD *and* RUSTAM *remain.*

RUSTAM: A Bahá'í home! I was born in a Bahá'í home, and because of that, the other children would throw stones at me. So they told me to swallow it, and that God was happy with that. I was thinking I'd like to pick up a rock and throw it back. So now I am here, I learn about freedom and justice, and if you throw stones at me, I take you to court, and you can't say it's because I'm a Bahá'í. Here, we have freedom and law—you want something, you work. You don't bribe someone or pray to someone. You want a TV and it costs $500, you go earn $500 and you got a TV. No one price for Muslims, one price for Bahá'ís. If I want to drink alcohol, I have to pay for the alcohol. I have to pay when I wake up the next morning. (*He laughs.*) This is freedom.

MELINDA: What's going on out here?

RUSTAM: We're getting ready for a wedding!

MELINDA: Is the food ready?

RUSTAM: Oh, it's ready all right.

ACT 1, SCENE 2

MELINDA: Well, we should be right out. (*She closes the door.*)

RUSTAM: It might be a little crispy. (*Hears baby's cry*) Daddy's coming, Parvaneh! Mommy's out with another man.

CHAD: So Bahá'ís don't drink, right? That's what Chris told me.

RUSTAM smiles and shakes his head and exits. CHRIS *enters carrying a big plate of cooked food and heads for the kitchen.*

CHRIS: What is going on this afternoon? It's like love just bouncing all over the place—I really need to say a prayer.

CHAD: Chris, I think maybe it's time for me to go home.

CHRIS: Oh, well, you want to eat first? It's not all burned.

The UR door opens, and the four parents enter, chatting.

MELINDA: Time to eat! What's going on outside?

MELINDA *places the bowl with the stones on the coffee table.* MR. SOBHANI *pats* CHRIS *on the shoulder.* CHRIS *goes to look in the bowl. All but he and* MELINDA *have exited,* CHAD *having gone into the bathroom.*

CHRIS: Do I see four stones in the bowl?!

MELINDA: Hold your horses, Kemosabe, I just put them in there to move them.

CHRIS: Very well. (*He carefully takes out the stones, placing them one by one on the table.*)

RUSTAM: (*Entering from bedroom, with baby.*) Time to eat, Africa.

CHRIS: I'll be right out.

RUSTAM *exits.* CHRIS *uses this diversion to get away from* MELINDA.

MELINDA: Are you angry you don't have your consent already?

CHRIS: I just need a minute.

MELINDA: So is this Semowa or Chris? 'Cause the Chris I knew hated when he didn't get exactly what he wanted when he wanted.

CHRIS: Are you here to mock my spiritual transformation?

MELINDA: No, I'm here getting the potato salad. Anyway, none of it matters unless you found him.

CHRIS: (*Low.*) Just do your part, that's all.

MELINDA: You know what my part is? All of it. Because I've always had to do all of it. Now God gave me the part of looking out for you at a time when you don't know up from down.

CHRIS: Look, I think you're misreading what's going on with me right now, but uh... this idea that since I am in love, I am no longer an adult, able to make critical decisions about my own life... Consent is about unity, not control.

MELINDA: No, not control, but that I need to use the wisdom of my years to help you.

CHRIS: Phhh.

MELINDA: You think that I am trying to wreck your life?

CHRIS: Don't you see, this is the same shit your mother done to you.

MELINDA: Don't talk like you're from the ghetto.

CHRIS: I speak the way I need to speak.

MELINDA: Oh right, the little black boy wandering the world looking for a home...

CHRIS: (*Overlapping.*) Not a boy, a MAN going out to make a new home...

MELINDA: (*Overlapping.*) ....And he thinks he's found it in some Persian girl's...

CHRIS: (*Overlapping.*) ...but his MOTHER won't let go of him!

MELINDA: This is not about my letting go. This is about you needing consent from both biological parents! I look around—someone is missing.

CHRIS: Enough! I found my father, okay?

A beat.

MELINDA: And?

CHRIS: And I am going to discuss the subject with the LSA at the appropriate time

ACT 1, SCENE 2

MELINDA: What does that mean? He said no?

CHAD *enters, stops.*

CHRIS: (*Trying to diffuse the situation.*) Mom, I've got it under control.

MELINDA: So you're going to try to get around it, huh? Go to them with some cry-baby story about how your father left you when you were young, and ask them to declare him a 'non-parent' or whatever they call it, like he's a child molester. I'm sorry that this law is hard and it falls harder on some than others, but it's there for a reason, and this is a spiritual test, my friend—a big one you are screwing with here.

CHAD *exits back into the bathroom.*

CHRIS: Are you through?

MELINDA: Your father struggled to stay alive in this country and I wouldn't go to Africa—that's the story! And you may be able to fool the majority on that LSA just so you can get what you want just like you always do! But God sees into your heart and He will judge all of us.

CHRIS: Are you through now?

MELINDA: Your father is a noble human being and you are tied to him in ways you don't understand, and you'd throw him away just like—God, I'm so mad I can't even look at you.

CHRIS: (*Almost devoid of feeling.*) Mom, the man I found was nothing but another nigger in the bush.

She throws the nearest object (a bowl of potato salad) at him. It misses and flies into the bathroom. Out of the bathroom comes CHAD, *shell-shocked, with potato salad on his clothes and in his hair.* MELINDA *and* CHRIS, *locked in a stare, give little sign of seeing this.* CHAD *collects his things.*

CHAD: Please, I just want to go home.

CHRIS: (*Breaking away from his mother.*) Sure. (*He speaks as if to ask* MELINDA *if she's proud of herself.*) I'll get the keys from Hal.

CHRIS *and* CHAD *walk out. End of scene.*

End of Act I

> "The Lord hath ordained that in every city a House of Justice be established wherein shall gather counsellors to the number of Bahá (9) ... It is incumbent upon them to take counsel together and to have regard for the interests of the servants of God, for His sake, even as they regard their own interests..."
>
> —Bahá'u'lláh

ACT II, Scene 1

The Sobhani home, toward evening. MR. *and* MRS. SOBHANI, HAL *and* MELINDA, NURA *and* TAHIRIH *are sitting in the living room at prayer. The scene begins with* MRS. SOBHANI *chanting a prayer in Persian. The prayer is about the heartbreak the lovers of God must face, and she chants it out of her own heartbreak. When she finishes,* HAL *speaks as if he has the floor.*

HAL: The nightingale in our midst... Well, friends, the Spiritual Assembly of Palm Terrace is open for business.

There is muted celebration.

HAL: So what is our agenda?

CHRIS *enters, through front door.*

HAL: Hey the cat came back.

CHRIS: I was trying to talk to him. He was pretty shut down. (*Hands keys to* HAL.)

MR. SOBHANI: It is true he has cancer?

HAL: He has Hodgkin's disease, which is a kind of lymphoma.

CHRIS: What'd I miss?

TAHIRIH: We ate.

HAL: We also elected officers. You're recording secretary. (*He throws a pad of paper and a pen in front of* CHRIS.)

CHRIS: Okay.

TAHIRIH: Hal is chair, I'm vice chair. My dad is treasurer, and your mom is secretary.

MELINDA: (*To no one in particular.*) Surprise.

RUSTAM *opens the door to their bedroom. A TV is on inside.*

RUSTAM: Nura! Ba<u>ch</u>che dáre gerye míkone.   نورا، بچه داره گریه می‌کنه.

[*Trans: The baby's crying.*]

He closes the door. NURA *ignores this.*

CHRIS: Is Rustam coming?

NURA: One of us needs to watch the baby—

HAL: And our ninth member, Joannie, has signaled she won't be attending.

CHRIS: So what happened with the neighbor?

The SOBHANIS *are silent.*

HAL: He settled down after a while—so just curious, how many of us have served on Assemblies?

Only HAL *and* MELINDA *raise their hands.*

HAL: Just the two of us? Cyrus?

MR. SOBHANI: In Iran, after Revolution, all Assemblies were stop.

HAL: I guess I knew that, but we just assume that the Persian friends understand these things. Maybe what we can do is set aside time at the beginning…

RUSTAM: (*Opens the door again and stares.*) Nura!

NURA: Sorry, just a moment. (*She gets up to go.*)

TAHIRIH: Haqq nadárí berí píshesh.   حق نداری بری پیشش.

[*Trans: Don't you dare go.*]

MR. SOBHANI: (*To* TAHIRIH.) Ehterám   احترام محفل را

mahfel-rá negah dár. ذگه دار.

[*Trans: Show respect to the Assembly.*]

NURA *closes the door. We then hear her raised voice rebuking* RUSTAM.

MELINDA: Should we wait?

The SOBHANIS *are mortified.* NURA *reenters, with the slightest air of triumph.*

TAHIRIH: (*Low.*) Áfarín. [*Trans: Well done.*] آفرین.

MELINDA: (*To* NURA.) Maybe the baby can sleep out here with us?

MR. SOBHANI: I think best is if we go on.

HAL: Maybe we can start by reading out of the manual.

MELINDA: The first agenda item should always be teaching, that's what the Guardian said.

CHRIS: That would be great if our only seeker hadn't run away.

MELINDA: He's not the only seeker, and he's got issues we're not ready for.

CHRIS: Cancer?

MELINDA: Not just that. Issues of neglect… His grandmother is a saint, but the parents are a mess.

CHRIS: We teach the grandmother then.

HAL: She's a diehard Christian.

TAHIRIH: We need to focus our efforts on people who are stable out there, like on the University campus.

CHRIS: We have no idea who Bahá'u'lláh has prepared to enter His Cause.

TAHIRIH: Chad is obviously not prepared—he ran away.

CHRIS: Covered in potato salad.

HAL: He was probably just run down. Maybe Nura would read this paragraph…

HAL *passes the manual to* NURA, *who looks a bit hesitant. At that moment,* RUSTAM *throws the bedroom door open and heads for the front door.*

NURA: Kojá mírí? کجا میری؟
   [*Trans: Where are you going?*]
RUSTAM: (*At door.*) OUT!
   He is gone. NURA *goes to the bedroom, trying to maintain her composure.*
NURA: (*Exiting.*) So sorry.
MR. SOBHANI: Tahirih-ján, maybe you read instead?
TAHIRIH: (*Taking manual.*) I need to read it once to myself.
CHRIS: While she's doing that—I don't know where it would fit on the agenda, but I'm a little anxious to get something out of the way on our consent.
MELINDA: Oh boy.
CHRIS: (*Pulls out a folded piece of paper.*) This is consent from my father.
TAHIRIH: Let me see?
MELINDA: You didn't tell me you had that.
CHRIS: I told you I had it under control.
TAHIRIH: Did you get chocolate on it?
CHRIS: Uh, no… that's blood.
   Silence.
HAL: This is voluntary consent?
CHRIS: Maybe we should put it down for later…
HAL: We're not getting that snake back in the can.
CHRIS: Look, it's not a big deal—
HAL: The floor is yours.
CHRIS: Okay, he stays in a little village called Maseru, it's in the Kalahari, hours from a paved road—I tracked him down and told him who I was. At first, he didn't let on. He just kept trying to make everyone laugh, the other guys hanging around, talking about how the chickens and goats were his only children.
MELINDA: He said that?

CHRIS: I didn't jump in the cooking pot, I didn't fill his belly. It made me laugh too, til I had time to think about it.

MELINDA: That's your father.

CHRIS: He didn't welcome me, didn't register any surprise I had shown up, come across the ocean and desert to see him— just a bunch of jokes.

HAL: So you killed him?

MELINDA: Hal!

CHRIS: Yeah. No, I just figured I'd get his consent and go. Had the paper ready, all he had to do was sign, but he wouldn't.

HAL: So then you killed him.

MELINDA: You're supposed to be setting an example how to act in LSA.

CHRIS: So he said do what I like, it had nothing to do with him.

MR. SOBHANI: Excuse me, he knows about Bahá'í law?

MELINDA: Sure he does, he's a Bahá'í himself.

CHRIS: Yeah, I asked him about that.

MELINDA: Of course he is.

CHRIS: The man I found was not the same man who left us eighteen years ago. He was… dirty… drunk.

MELINDA *groans*.

CHRIS: I had prepared a whole speech, but it just seemed wasted. So I told him he could sign it or not. If he didn't, I could either never get married, ever, or I could turn his name over to the Universal House of Justice and appeal that he be declared a 'non parent.'

HAL: They do that?

CHRIS: Anyway, he didn't like that at all, so he took the paper and pen, like it was always his idea, and what was her name, and how he always thought the Persians were a beautiful people…

MELINDA: (*Low.*) That's great, seeing as it was the Persians who were such a test.

ACT 2, SCENE 1   153

CHRIS: And he signed.

HAL: And the blood?

CHRIS: Well, I figured I was done so I walked away, and I got—I don't know—twenty feet when I feel him grab my arm, then he's got me by both arms. He didn't say anything—I don't know if he knew what he was doing—he's just staring into my eyes, breathing on me. I didn't fight him off—all this anger rising up inside, I had to let it go. I had prayed and prayed about this, asking God to help me not to hate him, not to hurt him, only to seek what was my right. And I felt myself opening up to what he was feeling, to his rage: Life has no meaning for him. And this feeling, this overwhelming sympathy, bubbling up from my chest and I think it must have shown, because he let go of my arms and started to laugh. But I just keep looking into his eyes—maybe he would see my victory, maybe this would help him. But then he holds up his hands, covered in blood. And he grabs the paper from me, wipes his hand on it, says, "THAT is my signature," and walks away.

TAHIRIH: So whose blood is this?

CHRIS: It's mine. (*He rolls up his sleeves to show scars on his biceps.*) His nails had broken my skin.

TAHIRIH: So this is why you're covering up?

MELINDA: You have scars.

HAL: So Chris, what sort of condition was your father in health-wise?

CHRIS: Yeah, right, that's what I was thinking, believe me.

MELINDA: O my God.

CHRIS: Look I had a test. It came back negative.

TAHIRIH: Doesn't it take a while?

CHRIS: 3 months to develop the HIV antibodies. I had it done at 3 months and at 6 months—I'm fine.

There is some relief.

CHRIS: Now you understand why I didn't want to open this can of worms early.

TAHIRIH: This letter is dated October 10.

CHRIS: Yeah.

TAHIRIH: We didn't talk about marriage until December.

CHRIS: Well, I wasn't sure the next time I'd be in his neighborhood.

TAHIRIH: But how did you know you'd need consent?

CHRIS: I mean, I knew where we were going with this.

TAHIRIH: Oh.

CHRIS: It's not a big deal.

TAHIRIH: Sure, and if it doesn't work out with me, you just cross out my name and write down the next girl's.

CHRIS: Maybe we can go to the next thing.

MELINDA: *(Paper in hand.)* So can we even accept this?

HAL: The date is more a technicality—

MELINDA: It doesn't appear so to Tahirih.

HAL: —now letters signed in blood, we may want to check the manual.

TAHIRIH: *(Standing.)* I'm sorry, I need to excuse myself for a minute.

MELINDA: *(To* HAL.*)* You just don't know when to stop.

CHRIS: Tahirih.

TAHIRIH: I'm fine, just go on—I'm sure you know everything I will say anyway.

She exits through UR *door,* CHRIS*'s heart going with her. A beat.*

MELINDA: Is someone going to read the quote?

HAL: Chris?

CHRIS: I'm sorry, I feel like I need to go to her.

MELINDA: We'll lose our quorum.

CHRIS: Oh—just give me a minute.

He goes to her door, knocks and goes in. The four parents are seated just as they were in the previous scene.

HAL: This feels familiar. You think they planned this time?

MELINDA: Don't be stupid.

HAL: Do you say that as an Assembly member or as a spouse? (*To* SOBHANIS.) Since we're only four, we can't make any decisions.

MRS. SOBHANI: Yes.

HAL: So I suggest we have ourselves another piece of baklava.

MELINDA: Half a piece.

MRS. SOBHANI: Tahirih just upset.

MELINDA: She should be praised for showing such restraint.

NURA: (*Poking in head.*) Sorry, five minutes.

MRS. SOBHANI: Not Chris—just argue with sister.

MR. SOBHANI: Hal and Melinda, I do something might surprise. (*He picks up a stone and puts it into the bowl.*)

MELINDA: Are you doing that for real?

MR. SOBHANI: Yes. I believe they are good bet.

MRS. SOBHANI *looks surprised as well.*

MELINDA: Sorry, didn't you see what a doofus he just was?

MR. SOBHANI: I think your son, he has good heart. He cares for my daughter. (*Laughs.*) He went to end of earth, faced biggest fear. I believe he works very hard to make him happy.

MELINDA: Make himself happy?

MRS. SOBHANI: Her.

MR. SOBHANI: Sorry... make her happy.

MELINDA: But they're just kids: 21, 22... I know age is not supposed to be the issue, but they don't have jobs!

HAL: But then neither do we.

MELINDA: That's different. Come on, Hal, that's beside the point!

HAL: Well, for what it's worth... I'll ante up too.

HAL *puts his stone in the bowl; he and* MR. SOBHANI *seem relieved and the pressure seems to have shifted to the mothers.* MELINDA *shakes her head, unconvinced.*

MELINDA: I just... (*grumbles*) ugh!

MRS. SOBHANI: Sorry... always I think Tahirih marry Persian. Always I think this. I grow Iran, Sirus grow Iran. Always we circle...

    Eháteh, chi mishe?   احاطه چی میشه؟

    [*Trans: How do you say 'surrounded'?*]

MR. SOBHANI: Surround.

MRS. SOBHANI: Always we surround Iranian. No think marry American white, American black. No Chris, John, Mike... Nah! Think Dariush, Mehrdad, Hasan, see? Always think Iranian girl need Iranian man.

MELINDA: That's hardly true.

MRS. SOBHANI: But always I think. Always watch TV, Iran, "COPS"—you know COPS? American always fight, always police. American black always gun, drug. I come America, I see black, I afraid. I look, have gun? Drug?

MELINDA: That's just so wrong.

MRS. SOBHANI: Yes, wrong. Still I afraid.

MELINDA: Parvin, you can't judge Chris by what you saw on COPS.

HAL: Let her speak, Melinda.

MRS. SOBHANI: Chris, no. Very good boy, kind, big smile always. But always I think Persian man for Persian girl. Number one: language. Imagine try to run house speak like me... uh, eh, oh, ptew...

    HAL *laughs*.

MELINDA: But Tahirih's English is very good.

MRS. SOBHANI: Yes, English good—Persian now bad. Number two:

    Farhang, chí míshe?   فرهنگ، چی میشه؟

    [*Trans: How do you say 'culture'?*]

MR. SOBHANI: Culture.

MRS. SOBHANI: Culture. In the Iran, the man he do like this, the girl she do like that. One understand other. Good, easy live together. Make family happy. Be <u>Khodá</u>! This is my big desire, to see children happy.

MELINDA: You don't think he would make her happy?

MRS. SOBHANI: I know he make her happy. I know he do.

(*Moved.*) Ay Jamál-i-Mubárak,   ای جمال مبارک،
komakeshún kon!   کمکشون کن!
Khoshbakhteshún kon!   خوشبختشون کن!
[*Trans: O Blessed Beauty! Help them! Bless them!*]

MELINDA: What did she say?

MR. SOBHANI: She ask Bahá'u'lláh to help them.

A beat. MELINDA *is moved as well.*

MELINDA: I'm so grateful to you for that, Parvin.

She reaches for MRS. SOBHANI's *hand. After a beat, she withdraws it.*

MRS. SOBHANI: Melinda, Hal, for me, family very important. Maybe for American, I think not important, but me, very important! If marry, family of Chris, family of Tahirih, one family. (*Gestures with hands coming together.*) Our daughter, the other, her husband, his family… they nice, but they not family, they (*gestures*) separate and is problem.

MELINDA: You're absolutely right. We need to be unified if they're going to make it.

MRS. SOBHANI: They family say they Bahá'í, I don't know…

MR. SOBHANI: They are Bahá'ís, maybe just not deepen.

MRS. SOBHANI: Just <u>name</u> Bahá'í.

MR. SOBHANI: Mohem níst.   مهم نیست.
[*Trans: It's not important.*]

MRS. SOBHANI: (*To* MR. SOBHANI.) Níst?   نیست؟ تربیت
Tarbíyat-e-rohaní nadáre! Man, báyad   روحانی نداره! من
be khánevádé-ash zang bezanam,   باید به خانوادهاش

begam: "Rustam bad raftárí, míkone, bíyáyíd harf bezaníd báhásh," valí nah! Moshkel-e-má-st!   زنگ بزنم، بگم: >>رستم بد رفتاری میکنه، بیایید حرف بزنید باهاش، << ولی نه! مشکل ماست!

[Trans: *It's not? He has no morals! I should be able to call his family and tell them: "Rustam is behaving badly, come talk to him," but no! He's our problem!*]

MR. SOBHANI: Chris mesle-ún níst.   کریس مثل اون نیست.

[Trans: *Chris is not the same.*]

MRS. SOBHANI: Valí aqallan zabun-eshún mífahmam! Ínhá khárejí-and...   ولی اقلا زبونشون میفهمم! اینها خارجی اند...

[Trans: *But at least I can speak their language! These are non-Persians...*]

MR. SOBHANI: Ajeleh nakon.   عجله نکن.

[Trans: *Take your time. (i.e., with deciding on consent.)*]

MELINDA: (*Getting up.*) Well, that does it for me for tonight. I don't know what you were saying in Persian, but the English made sense.

HAL: The meeting's not adjourned.

MELINDA: (*Exiting.*) Thank you for dinner.

HAL *is perturbed and exhales.* NURA *enters from the downstage bedroom.*

NURA: Sorry, I think she will sleep now. Where is everybody?

TAHIRIH *enters abruptly, heads to the bathroom without acknowledging the others.* NURA, *concerned, follows after her.* CHRIS *enters, looking pensive.*

HAL: Check it out. (*He holds up the bowl.*) Only two to go, chief!

CHRIS: She won't even talk to me. (*Takes bowl.*) Maybe I can tell her.

MR. SOBHANI: Wait, Chris, Semowa, come. (*He sits* CHRIS *between himself and his wife.*)

CHRIS: Maybe it would, you know...

MR. SOBHANI: Everything you cannot repair. Sometimes it just is broken, so you clean up and you wait.

The baby is heard crying. MRS. SOBHANI *gets up to go.*

MRS. SOBHANI: Tahirih be okay.

It's now just the three men, who sit in silence a moment.

HAL: You missed it, Chris. You really had something going in here— We could see it before our eyes, like two houses becoming one.

MR. SOBHANI: Two houses becoming one.

End of scene.

"O people of the world! Follow not the promptings of the self, for it summoneth insistently to wickedness and lust; follow, rather, Him Who is the Possessor of all created things, Who biddeth you to show forth piety, and manifest the fear of God."

—Bahá'u'lláh

ACT II, Scene 2

It's nighttime. TAHIRIH *and* NURA *are nestled in the couch, lit by the TV, which is playing a scary film (e.g., "The Sixth Sense").* TAHIRIH *is dejected, leaning away from* NURA, *who is half absorbed in the movie, half-attentive to* TAHIRIH.

NURA: Hey, you can't sleep. I'm not watching this alone.

TAHIRIH: I'm not sleeping.

NURA: Just call him. This is nothing.

TAHIRIH *doesn't respond.* NURA *shakes her head and turns her attention back to the movie.* KAYVAN *has tiptoed in from the* DR *door wearing pajamas and no socks. He taps* NURA *on the shoulder.*

KAYVAN: Nura?

NURA: (*Screams.*) WHAHH! Kayvan! (*Smacks him.*)

KAYVAN: Ow!

NURA: Posht-e saram dárí che kár míkoní?! پشت سرم داری چه کار می‌کنی؟!

[*Trans: What are you doing sneaking up behind me?!*]

TAHIRIH: Please be quiet!

MR. SOBHANI *enters from the DL door.*

MR. SOBHANI: Che tún-e? [*Trans: What's wrong?*] چتونه؟...

ACT 2, SCENE 2

(*To* KAYVAN.) Why aren't you in bed?

KAYVAN: I just wanted to ask her something.

MR. SOBHANI *exits.* HAL *enters from the DR door carrying a fastidiously compiled collection of his papers, which includes typed pages and scraps. He places this on a shelf.* NURA *notices that* KAYVAN *hasn't left.*

NURA: Go.

KAYVAN: I need to pee.

He lingers a bit behind the couch watching the movie, dancing. HAL *has walked over to the DL door, right past* KAYVAN. *Neither acknowledges the other's presence. This is the nature of the scene: we're watching events in both houses at the same time. Or more poetically, the two houses are become one.*

HAL: (*Opening the DL door.*) Hey…

MELINDA: (*Off, barely audible.*) I'm praying.

HAL: Are you finished? (*Goes in.*)

NURA *pauses the movie.*

NURA: You shouldn't be watching.

KAYVAN: I can't help it.

NURA: Boro! [*Trans: Get going!*]   برو!

He runs off to the bathroom. NURA *returns to the movie.* MELINDA *enters, pursued by* HAL.

MELINDA: It's so hot in here I'm going to explode!

HAL: (*Dancing.*) "When we kiss…woooo… Fire…"

MELINDA: Please, I'm sticky.

HAL: Okay, just this once. (*He flips on the air conditioning switch.*)

MELINDA: (*Grabbing a book to fan herself.*) Huuuh.

HAL: Why must you abuse my books?

MELINDA: So this is your book? Fine. (*She tosses the book at him and exits into the bedroom.*)

HAL: You think you're going to get my goat…

She shuts the door. He runs up to it and opens it. KAYVAN *runs out of the bathroom and almost collides with* HAL *on his way to the couch.*

MELINDA: (*Off.*) Ow! You hurt my hand!

HAL: What are you doing holding the door? (*He exits and closes the door behind him.*)

MELINDA: (*Off.*) Hal!

NURA *pauses the movie again.*

KAYVAN: Can I stay here?

NURA: I just put clean sheets on your bed.

KAYVAN: I can hear it anyway. It's worse because I'm alone in there.

NURA: I'll turn it down.

KAYVAN: Come on, Nura!

NURA: I'll lock you in the closet!

He runs off and slams the door. She waits.

NURA: Not behind the door. Bed.

KAYVAN: (*Right behind the door.*) I am!

She listens, and then turns the movie back on and lowers the volume. MELINDA *enters, followed by* HAL.

HAL: (*Playful.*) Don't just walk away—

MELINDA: I don't notice to tell you the truth.

HAL: I do.

MELINDA: That's because you're obsessed.

HAL: I'm obsessed?—because once a month I want to exercise my marriage privilege.

MELINDA *goes to the kitchen and begins piling up lemons on the counter. Throughout the following dialogue she cuts lemons and squeezes the juice into a pitcher.*

HAL: It's almost midnight.

MELINDA: If you're going to keep me up, I might as well get something accomplished.

HAL: You know, I'm always looking for some sort of insight into the way your mind works...

MELINDA: Try looking outside the gutter.

HAL: Did you ever think maybe God created sex for us to enjoy? And that's why things tingle the way they do?

MELINDA: Keep your voice down—

HAL: Chris knows what sex is—and he has the right to enjoy it too.

MELINDA: Now you're just trying to provoke me.

   KAYVAN *enters quietly, watches the movie from afar.*

MELINDA: I'll have you know—despite the fact that I could have chopped his head off today—part of me is rooting for them.

HAL: There you go, and you and Parvin seemed to be warming up a bit.

MELINDA: Another part of me is not so sure, and since this is the most important decision I've made since having him…

HAL: Why not just stop with this oedipal thing, give your blessing and let them have at it? (*He smiles devilishly.*)

   MELINDA *exhales—blowing off some steam—and then collects herself.*

MELINDA: It has been twenty-four hours—that implies no oedipal thing, thank you. God is my witness, I am only thinking of their happiness.

HAL: Admit it, Melinda, you have a problem with sex.

MELINDA: I'll tell you my problem with sex, Hal—I'll tell it to you straight. Sex should come out of <u>love</u> and <u>appreciation</u> that is mutual and spiritual.

HAL: Oh, I don't love you? I've spent my last 8 years proving my love to you. No, the issue here is sex!

   NURA *turns to see* KAYVAN *standing in the doorway.*

NURA: Eehh!

KAYVAN: I'm not watching.

NURA: (*Getting up.*) In the closet you go!

KAYVAN: (*Going back into his room.*) No. Nura, no!

   She chases him off. There's a struggle.

TAHIRIH: (*Sitting up.*) Nura, what are you doing?

> HAL *has come down to the shelf where he put his papers earlier. He takes the binder down to show to* MELINDA.

HAL: I will not have my bliss disturbed this evening. I just finished the outline AND organized all my ideas into twelve chapter headings. Now don't I deserve a treat?

MELINDA: Sure, have a lemon.

HAL: All I have to do now is write the thing—What? The preparation is the hardest part!

> *There is knocking and shouting off from Kayvan's room.* MELINDA *cocks her head as if she hears something from UL door.*

MELINDA: Did you hear something?

> NURA *enters.*

TAHIRIH: You locked him in the closet?

NURA: He has his blanket and his pillow, he's fine.

> MELINDA *crosses to the UL door (Chris's room) to listen.* NURA *starts the movie again, turns up the volume.* MR. SOBHANI *enters from the DL door.*

NURA: Sorry, Bábá, you don't need to come out if you hear something—It's just our movie.

MR. SOBHANI: Your mother is trying to sleep. (*Exits.*)

TAHIRIH: (*To* NURA.) You're sick.

NURA: He needs to learn.

TAHIRIH: You need to learn. Where is your husband tonight?

> *Nura's cell phone goes off. She pauses the movie.*

NURA: (*Feeling redeemed.*) I wonder who is that.

HAL: What are you doing?

MELINDA: (*Still at Chris's door.*) Shh.

> NURA *checks the incoming number and grimaces.*

NURA: (*Answering.*) Kayvan, why are you calling me?

TAHIRIH: (*Mocking.*) "I wonder who is that."

ACT 2, SCENE 2

NURA: You stay in there until I let you out.

HAL: Stop eavesdropping!

NURA: Kayvan, if you call again or hit on the wall, I am telling Chris you wet your bed.

TAHIRIH: You're such a witch.

NURA: Don't cry—I'll tell him!

MELINDA: I don't know if he's crying or praying.

NURA: If you are afraid, say prayer and God will help you.

NURA hangs up, turns the TV off, gets up and walks past MELINDA into the UL room. MELINDA shifts her focus back to HAL.

MELINDA: So how long until you're done?

HAL: The book?—six months, maybe a year.

MELINDA: See, I don't think you appreciate the urgency of our situation.

HAL: We're okay, we've got a roof—

MELINDA: For how long? If I could work, I would, but—

HAL: Your health.

MELINDA: Yes, my health!

HAL: I know, and I am working as hard as I can.

MELINDA: Make it easier on yourself: Take a job, give yourself a whole other year to do the book…

HAL: All that diffuse light I once spread over hundreds of needy youth, that don't listen anyway, now I'm focusing it like a laser beam on the real problem.

MELINDA: Which is…?

HAL: Which is materialism!

MELINDA: Of course! I don't know why I was thinking we could leave that to Bahá'u'lláh.

HAL: People don't understand Bahá'u'lláh's writings—they need clear cut instructions, put into easy categories with examples and stories and sifted data.

MELINDA: What if you can't find a publisher? Are you going to sell it out of the back of your car?

HAL: If it comes to that! I don't know what you understand of a mission, but I've got one.

MELINDA: No, we've got one—together. And this personal mission of yours is endangering it.

NURA *enters with the baby, who is making baby noises.*

HAL: Well, I'm sorry if I can't share the final fruit of it all yet, but I can't. (*He goes to open the front door, but it won't open.*)

NURA: Shh… Where's mommy?

HAL: You always turn it around and make me feel like the whole thing is my fault.

NURA: Boop. Parvaneh… zoo-zoo-zoo-zoo…

HAL: Gaaah!

He forces the door open, walks out and paces just outside, leaving the door open. NURA *exits out the front door, still gently shaking the baby.*

MELINDA: Still got that lock to fix.

HAL: This is why I don't want a house—they are the mother of all time suckers!

MELINDA: You are so ungrateful.

HAL: Melinda, I have one nerve left—stay off it!

MELINDA: Good, maybe you'll just unravel altogether and we can start over from scratch.

HAL: That's what you want!

MELINDA: What I want is a partner who appreciates his life and appreciates me!

HAL: I appreciate my life!

MELINDA: And?

HAL: And I'd appreciate if you'd give me a little room.

MELINDA: How much room do you need, Hal? I'll give you all the room you want!

A beat. NURA *comes back in with the baby.*

NURA: Mommy is not happy with Daddy.

MELINDA: You want to be single? Is that it?

HAL: No, I want to be free!

MELINDA: Oh, I've heard that one before.

NURA: (*At couch.*) Tahirih...

TAHIRIH *groans impatiently.*

NURA: Fine, sleep there.

HAL: Why won't you just listen and hear what I'm really trying to say, and not your own clouded translation of it?

MELINDA: How am I supposed to translate that?

HAL: Freedom! Think back when the air between us was light and warm. You remember that place? Why can't we find that again?

CHRIS *comes out of the UL bedroom, walks into the bathroom.* HAL *and* MELINDA *are quiet a moment.* NURA *has exited into the UL bedroom, locking the door.*

HAL: Look, you're my wife and I love that you are—It's not us, it's all of this stuff around us. (*Holding her close.*) You're the one thing I want to keep out of all of it. You—the real you— the you that only I really know, not this hypersensitive, hypoallergenic ball of complaints and ailments.

MELINDA: Excuse me?

HAL: I know you, that's not you.

MELINDA: (*After a beat.*) That was a pretty well-crafted phrase. Did you write that in your book?

HAL: Come on.

MELINDA: (*Moving away.*) I thought so.

HAL: You're missing the point.

MELINDA: No, I feel the point. (*She exits into the DL bedroom, closes the door.*)

HAL: Don't go in there! (*He tries the door, it's locked.*) GRRRRR!!

RUSTAM *walks through the front door, evidently in good humor. He doesn't see* TAHIRIH *on the couch.*

RUSTAM: (*To no one in particular.*) Hello.

HAL: Melinda, open up!

CHRIS: (*Reentering.*) Dude, what's going on?

HAL *walks away, back toward the DR door.* RUSTAM *goes to the UL door, which he tries and finds locked. He knocks lightly, pauses a moment there, and waits.*

HAL: (*Before leaving.*) There's a trick to marriage, Chris, and it's really quite simple: Give up your dreams, your goals, your mission—flush 'em all down the toilet, because it's impossible to keep them plus your marriage PLUS your sanity.

HAL *exits.* CHRIS *comes down and sits on the floor close to* TAHIRIH, *who still sleeps. He puts down his head as if trying to communicate across the distance.*

CHRIS: Oh Tahirih, can you hear me tonight?

RUSTAM *has given up waiting for* NURA *to open the door, and he prepares for another night on the couch. He sees* TAHIRIH *there and halts.*

RUSTAM: Hello.

He takes a moment to look at her. He sits on the other end of the couch at a respectable distance.

RUSTAM: You are here, on my second bed—why? (*He moves his head closer to her and breathes in.*) Mmm… If you knew how much I'm dreaming about you. Every night I tell myself no, but I can't hold myself.

He starts to massage her foot. Half asleep, TAHIRIH *responds positively to the massage, not realizing who is giving it.*

RUSTAM: (*Whispers.*) You like that?

He moves up her calf, sliding his hand inside her pajamas. This is no brotherly massage.

RUSTAM: How about up there?

TAHIRIH: (*Waking up.*) What are you doing?

RUSTAM: Just a massage.

ACT 2, SCENE 2

TAHIRIH: Get your hands off of me.

RUSTAM: Ssshhhh.

TAHIRIH: Don't shush me, I said no.

RUSTAM: You want to play?

He grabs her. She tries to fight him off, but he is stronger. He pushes her onto the couch and pins her arms.

RUSTAM: I know what you were doing, waiting for me out here.

TAHIRIH: Get off!

RUSTAM covers her mouth, and they struggle. NURA has entered to see this.

NURA: Rustam!

He stands up, stares at her. TAHIRIH slips off the couch and away.

RUSTAM: Hello dear, did we wake you?

NURA: What is this?

RUSTAM: Nothing, just playing around.

NURA: You liar! (*She starts to hit him.*)

RUSTAM: Calm down.

TAHIRIH: Stop, Nura—It's not his fault!

NURA: What?

RUSTAM: See!

TAHIRIH: It's your fault. You knew what he was and you refused to kick the animal out.

RUSTAM: You watch your mouth.

TAHIRIH: You're not going to touch me. (*To* NURA.) I don't want to see him again, not here, not at the store…

RUSTAM: They are not your decisions to make.

TAHIRIH: Calling the police and reporting sexual assault is my decision the next time I see you. (*To* NURA.) You have to make a choice: him or us!

She takes some car keys, walks out the front door still in her pajamas.

NURA: Where are you going? Tahirih!

She runs out. The car is heard starting and leaving. Meanwhile, HAL *has entered with a paper shredder, which he has plugged in and placed on a table, close to their bedroom. He retrieves his binder.*

HAL: Melinda, you may want to come out and watch this! Sorry, Chris, if this is a little loud.

He opens his binder and takes a deep breath. NURA *reenters.*

NURA: *(To* RUSTAM.*)* What have you done?!

She exits into the bathroom. He sits down on the couch and turns on the TV.

RUSTAM: Yeah, go cry yourself!

MR. SOBHANI: *(Entering.)* What is going on out here?

RUSTAM: You have very emotional daughters.

HAL: Okay: Outline, page 1! *(He shreds the paper.)*

MR. SOBHANI: Who is crying in there? *(Knocking on the bathroom door.)* Nura?

HAL: Outline, page 2! *(Shreds it.)* Hear that, Melinda?! That is the sound of my mission… dying!

The DL door opens, MRS. SOBHANI *comes out.*

MRS. SOBHANI: Chí shode? چی شده؟

[*Trans: What happened?*]

MR. SOBHANI: Go in and talk to Nura.

MRS. SOBHANI: Nura-ján, dar-o báz kon. *(She goes in.)* [*Trans: Open the door.*] نورا جان، درو باز کن.

HAL: Okay, you don't care, SO—outline, pages 3, 4, 5 and 6! *(Shreds it and cries out with the pain of losing it.)* AAAAhhhhh!

CHRIS: That's not your book?

HAL: *(Loud, so* MELINDA *can hear.)* Why, yes it is my book, Chris, that's why I'm shredding it! *(Pulls out some more paper.)*

MR. SOBHANI: Where is Tahirih?

RUSTAM: She went to bed.

MR. SOBHANI *takes a moment to watch* RUSTAM, *then goes out the UR door.*

ACT 2, SCENE 2

HAL: Okay, notes for Chapter 1! Page 1! (*Shreds it.*) Page 2! (*Shreds, winces.*) Page 3!

MELINDA *enters.*

MELINDA: What are you doing?

HAL: Just killing time, dear... (*Shreds.*)

MELINDA: You have that all on computer.

HAL: I had it, just deleted it not two minutes ago. (*Shreds.*)

MELINDA: You have it backed up?

HAL: All gone. (*Shreds.*)

MELINDA: Stop!

HAL: No dear, you need to feel appreciated. Page 7 (*Shreds.*)

MELINDA: Hal!

HAL: Eight!

MELINDA: Stop it!

MELINDA *picks up his binder and exits through the UR door.*

HAL: (*Following her out.*) Come back with that!

CHRIS: (*Emerging momentarily from his prayer.*) Why don't you two just let go?!

MR. SOBHANI *has entered from the same door.*

MR. SOBHANI: She's not there.

RUSTAM: I didn't say she was.

MR. SOBHANI: You said she went to bed.

RUSTAM: I didn't say in that bed—Check her black boy.

MR. SOBHANI: Bítarbíyat! Why are you not happy   [...] !بی تربیت just to live but you always must make trouble?!

[*Trans: How rude!*]

RUSTAM: Maybe because you push so hard to make me just like you!

After a beat, MR. SOBHANI *breaks from* RUSTAM *and knocks on the bathroom door. Meanwhile,* HAL *and* MELINDA *are heard off.*

MELINDA: (*Off.*) Stay away from me!

HAL: (*Off.*) Give it back!

CHRIS: Will you two please stop and take a minute?

MRS. SOBHANI *opens the bathroom door.*

MR. SOBHANI: Did she say where Tahirih is?

MRS. SOBHANI: No.

MR. SOBHANI: (*At Kayvan's door.*) Kayvan is not in his bed either.

RUSTAM: (*Up, having gathered some things.*) Yes, keep on puking, my love, it makes your breath so fragrant. Rustam is going on vacation—maybe I send a postcard!

He walks out the front door. MR. SOBHANI *goes to the door.*

MR. SOBHANI: Where are my children?!

A car is heard starting. NURA *enters, covering her mouth with a towel.* MRS. SOBHANI *follows after her.*

MRS. SOBHANI: Begu ke sálem-and. بگو که سالمند.

[*Trans: Just tell us they're safe.*]

NURA: (*Managing to speak.*) Kayvan's closet.

MRS. SOBHANI: Sírús, boro tú-ye سیروس، برو توی کمد

komod negáh kon. نگاه کن.

[*Trans: Go look in the closet!*]

MR. SOBHANI *goes quickly to DR door, exits.* MELINDA *and* HAL *are heard shouting off.*

MRS. SOBHANI: Tell me what happen.

CHRIS: God, help this family—hold us together.

MR. SOBHANI: (*Reentering.*) He is sleeping in his closet—why was the door lock?

MRS. SOBHANI: Táhirih kú? طاهره کو؟

[*Trans: Where is Tahirih?*]

NURA: Please, go to bed. Everything will be fine and Tahirih will come home. (*Runs back into the bathroom.*)

ACT 2, SCENE 2

MRS. SOBHANI: (*Going to* MR. SOBHANI.)

    Va-í, Sirus, negarán-esh-am.   وای، سیروس، نگرانشم.

    [*Trans: I'm worried for her.*]

MR. SOBHANI: (*Holding her.*) She will be okay.

    They sit on the couch. MELINDA *and* HAL *enter, hurriedly.*

MELINDA: You think this is what I want, for you to destroy your work?!

HAL: You need to know you're loved and appreciated.

MELINDA: I need to know that you're a part of this family, that you have a care for whether we're sinking—It's not the book, Hal, it's you! The book is just an excuse you have been using to get away from reality, and for months I've been wondering what is so bad about our lives that you have to slip out and I thought it might be the job or the move or living with my mother, but it's not. Now it's clear it's me. (*She puts down the binder and exits into the bedroom. Off.*) The hyper-critical… bunch of complaints, whatever it was. (*Reentering with a pocketbook and coat.*) I need to be away from here.

HAL: What?

CHRIS: Mom, where are you going?

MELINDA: We need some time to re-evaluate our relationship.

HAL: Melinda, don't walk out that door!

    She is out and closes the door. HAL *blows off some steam.*

HAL: She'll come right back. Where's she going to go?

    MRS. SOBHANI *begins to chant a prayer.* CHRIS *returns to an attitude of prayer, but* HAL *is still too emotional. He focuses his stare on the downstage lamp, and flicks the switch off and on nervously. There is a knock on the door.*

HAL: What did I tell you?

    He opens the door. TAHIRIH *is there, in her pajamas.*

TAHIRIH: (*Putting on a cheery face for* HAL.) Hi, I hope it's not too late for a visit.

HAL: Oh, hi. Chris? (*He gives them some room.*)

CHRIS: Heeeyyy, what are you doing here?

TAHIRIH: Can I use your phone?

CHRIS: Of course.

CHRIS *retrieves the phone for her.* *She dials, walks downstage for a little privacy to call. A cell phone is heard ringing faintly.*

CHRIS: Can I get you something?

TAHIRIH: (*Into phone.*) Kayván? Beba<u>kh</u>shíd. کیوان ، ببخشید.
 Mámán o bábá bídár-and? مامان و بابا بیدارند؟
 [*Trans: Sorry. Are mom and dad awake?*]

KAYVAN *enters with cell phone, as if just having woken.*

KAYVAN: Bábá, phone.

MR. SOBHANI *takes the phone and holds onto* KAYVAN *lovingly.*

MR. SOBHANI: (*Into phone.*) Tahirih-ján?

TAHIRIH: (*Into phone.*) Alláh-u-abhá, bábá.

KAYVAN: Let me go.

MR. SOBHANI: (*Into phone, not letting* KAYVAN *go.*)
 Alláh-u-abhá. Kojá hastí? الله ابهی. کجا هستی؟
 [*Trans: Where are you?*]

TAHIRIH: (*Into phone.*) Kháne-ye- خانه کریس. همچی خوبه.
 Chris. Hamechí-khúb-e.
 [*Trans: Chris' house. Everything is fine.*]

MR. SOBHANI: (*Into phone.*) Khodá-rá shokr! خدا را شکر! طاهره،
 Táhirih, emshab che khabar shode? امشب چه خبر شده؟
 [*Trans: Thank God! What happened tonight?*]

TAHIRIH *doesn't respond.*

HAL: (*To* CHRIS.) I think I'm going to walk a bit. She'll be back once she cools off. (*He leaves.*)

TAHIRIH: (*Into phone.*) I'll be okay.

MR. SOBHANI: (*Into phone.*) Kay míyá-í? کی میای؟

ACT 2, SCENE 2

[*Trans: When are you coming?*]

TAHIRIH: (*Into phone.*) Nemíyám, nah tá vaqtí ke ú narafte...   نمی‌ایم، نه تا وقتی که او نرفته ...

[*Trans: I'm not, not until he's gone.*]

MR. SOBHANI: (*Into phone.*) Chí mígí?   چی میگی؟

[*Trans: What do you mean?*]

TAHIRIH: (*Into phone.*) My sister's husband—ask her. Emshab, rúye mobl-e Chris míkhábam.   امشب، روی مبل کریس می‌خوابم.

[*Trans: I'll sleep on Chris' couch tonight.*]

MR. SOBHANI: (*Into phone.*) Tahirih, you can tell us anything.

TAHIRIH: (*Into phone.*) It's Nura's turn. I'll call tomorrow.

She hangs up the phone. CHRIS *has gone to get something.* MR. SOBHANI *hugs his wife and* KAYVAN, *who squirms.*

MRS. SOBHANI: What he did?

MR. SOBHANI: She won't say. She's with Chris. I think she is okay. We raise her right...

MRS. SOBHANI: I not worry about Chris, but Rustam! I don't want here no more.

MR. SOBHANI: All we know is they were arguing.

MRS. SOBHANI: No, no, this more. You want, fine—he come back, he your problem! (*She exits.*)

KAYVAN: Can I go now?

He leaves. MR. SOBHANI *wanders a bit, then exits.* CHRIS *has reentered with a blanket, which he places on* TAHIRIH's *shoulders.*

CHRIS: I'm so happy to see you.

TAHIRIH: Sit down Chris, we gotta talk.

She has his attention.

TAHIRIH: I'm not sure this is going to work.

CHRIS: This?

TAHIRIH: Us. Marriage.

CHRIS: Okay.

TAHIRIH: Do you have any response to that?

CHRIS: I made a mistake—

TAHIRIH: I thought we knew each other—I thought we agreed to respect each other and tell the truth about everything, but maybe you think I'm just some Persian wife, and you can control what I say or do…

CHRIS: Of course not.

TAHIRIH: You wouldn't listen to what I was saying about Chad, you stop me from making a trade with your mom, and apparently we're engaged because you decided so, and I find this out where? In front of everyone.

CHRIS: That's not true.

TAHIRIH: Again with the discounting of what I'm saying! You hug me in front of my family after I ask you not to. You think I say these things for no reason?

CHRIS: What's going on?

TAHIRIH: Why is there something going on with me?

CHRIS: You're here at midnight in your pajamas.

TAHIRIH: Maybe I won't tell you—at least for six months, and then I'll let everyone in both families know at the same time.

CHRIS: Okay, I guess I deserve that.

TAHIRIH: I just wonder what other secrets are waiting to come up.

CHRIS: Don't you know how I feel about you?

TAHIRIH: Feelings change! Before they were married, Rustam would do anything for Nura, walk hours just to see her.

CHRIS: You think I might end up like him?

She doesn't answer.

CHRIS: Listen, the consent of our parents is second—you and I have to commit first.

TAHIRIH: I want a guarantee that it won't end badly.

ACT 2, SCENE 2

CHRIS: I can't give you that.

TAHIRIH: Then let's call it off.

A beat.

CHRIS: All along, this is what I've been most afraid of: that you were just this supreme test God had prepared, that I would have to let go of you, and that you would never really love me.

TAHIRIH: No, no, no, that is not the issue!—You bonehead, if I wanted to marry someone I didn't love, I'd at least find some doctor who drives a BMW.

CHRIS: Not an artist?

TAHIRIH: Who can't even give me a gold ring!

CHRIS: Well, I love you too.

TAHIRIH: Well duh. (*A beat.*) Don't look so serious, Semowa, it doesn't suit you.

CHRIS: She called me Semowa.

TAHIRIH: That's your name, isn't it? I told my Dad I was going to sleep on your couch.

CHRIS: Can you tell me what happened?

TAHIRIH: No. You'll just have to trust that, like I'll have to trust you couldn't tell me about your father.

CHRIS: Okay. Well, we don't have a couch, but you can sleep in my bed.

She looks at him. He smiles.

CHRIS: I'll sleep out here. Thanks to Mother Africa, I can sleep anywhere.

TAHIRIH: Okay.

CHRIS: And in the morning... French toast?

TAHIRIH: Okay. (*She walks to the UL door.*) I imagined our first night together would be different.

CHRIS: Yeah. Wait, what did you imagine?

TAHIRIH: Sweet dreams. (*She exits, closes the door.*)

CHRIS *settles into the reclining chair, and then shakes his head. A knock. The door opens and* MELINDA *is there.* CHRIS *doesn't notice.*

MELINDA: Hello? Cyrus, Parvin?

NURA: (*Entering, with baby.*) Melinda?

MELINDA: I'm sorry, I didn't know where else to go.

NURA: Please come and sit.

MELINDA: I'm sorry to wake you up.

NURA: Can I get you something?

MELINDA: No thanks… (*She begins to tear up.*) Maybe I can just sit on your couch a few minutes.

NURA: Of course.

MELINDA: (*Touching baby's head.*) She's so sweet.

NURA: She was to bring us together.

MRS. SOBHANI *enters.*

MRS. SOBHANI: What happen?

MELINDA: Sorry, Parvin. Nura told me I could sit here.

MRS. SOBHANI: What is it?

MELINDA: Nothing—just… I don't know where I am. I have no friends. I didn't know where to go until I found myself pulling into your drive, hoping you'd be awake. I just feel very alone in the world. (*Picks up one of the consent stones from the table.*) Like a little rock floating out in space. But you don't know what I'm talking about.

MRS. SOBHANI: I understand alone.

A beat.

MELINDA: Maybe I'll go.

MRS. SOBHANI: You not alone (*She picks up the other stone and touches Melinda's stone with it.*) We family.

End of Scene.

"Truly, the Lord loveth union and harmony and abhorreth separation and divorce. Live ye one with another, O people, in radiance and joy. By My life! All that are on earth shall pass away, while good deeds alone shall endure… Compose your differences, O My servants; then heed ye the admonition of Our Pen of Glory and follow not the arrogant and wayward."

—Bahá'u'lláh

ACT II, Scene 3

The scene opens on the Sobhani home just before Tahirih and Chris's wedding, which is happening in a tent in the backyard. The doorbell rings. MR. SOBHANI *enters from the kitchen area, finishing a conversation on the telephone with relatives in Iran. He opens the door to find a large display of flowers. No one is there, so he brings the flowers in, still talking on the phone.* KAYVAN *enters from the DL door, wearing a hat.*

KAYVAN: Dad, can I ride in the car with Tahirih and Chris to the hotel tonight?

MR. SOBHANI: Why do you ask me this?

KAYVAN: Semowa said yes, but Tahirih said it was past my bedtime.

MR. SOBHANI: Men stay up late, boys do not. Show me today a young man and you stay late, okay?

 KAYVAN *starts jumping up and down.*

MR. SOBHANI: You have the rings?

KAYVAN: They're in my coat.

MR. SOBHANI: Make sure—Wait, why are you wearing that hat?

KAYVAN: We did my hair like Chris's. I was going to keep this on until it was too late for Mámán to say anything.

MR. SOBHANI: Good thinking.

KAYVAN *exits.* HAL *enters through the front door. He is perspiring.*

HAL: Your wife is a real general—I've never seen this side of her.

MR. SOBHANI: You believed the man rule Persian house?

HAL: She's trying to save that cake from melting, but it ain't happenin'. (*Knocks on DR door.*) Ten minutes to show time!

MR. SOBHANI: How's the tent?

HAL: (*Knocks on DL door.*) Ten minutes, ladies! (*To* MR. SOBHANI.) It would be fine if they'd keep the flaps closed—

MR. SOBHANI: And the guests?

HAL: Noisy—There's gotta be a hundred-fifty Persians out there. God help us if all that makeup starts to melt. Cyrus, we appreciate you doing all this. Chris told me it's not the custom for the family of the bride.

MR. SOBHANI: We are happy.

HAL: Is Melinda here yet?

MR. SOBHANI: Yes, in Tahirih's room.

HAL: I don't know if you know, she's been staying with her mother.

MR. SOBHANI: How is it for you?

HAL: You trade in one sort of pain for another that's worse.

The phone rings. MR. SOBHANI *keeps focused on* HAL.

HAL: You want to get that?

MR. SOBHANI: Sorry. (*Answers.*) Hello. Alláh-u-abhá, Kamran-ján...

NURA: (*Poking her head in from DL door, whispering.*) Kí-e?   کیه

[*Trans: Who is it?*]

MR. SOBHANI *shakes his head and retreats to the kitchen.* NURA *exits.* MELINDA *has entered from* UR *door.*

MELINDA: Look at those flowers, aren't they lovely? Hi Hal.

HAL: Hey there. People are asking about you out there.

MELINDA: That's why I'm in here. (*Heading towards bathroom.*)

HAL: (*Reaching.*) A letter came... for Chris. I keep forgetting—How are you?

MELINDA: I'm patient. (*Exiting.*) Hope I can say the same for you.

MR. SOBHANI: (*Reentering, still on phone.*) Go right at second traffic lights.

A knock at the door. HAL *gestures to* MR. SOBHANI *that he will get it. He opens the door and* CHAD *is there dressed in his church clothes.*

HAL: Hey, Chad. Hot out there, eh?

CHAD: It's the sun mostly. Can I sit in here?

MR. SOBHANI: (*Still on phone.*) Pass the river, then make U-turn. (*He pats* CHAD *on the back.*)

HAL: (*Exiting.*) Tell them your front yard looks like a car lot for Lexus.

MR. SOBHANI: (*He hangs up. To* CHAD.) It's so good you are here to my home again.

CHAD: I was invited.

MR. SOBHANI: Of course.

KAYVAN *has entered and he hands his father a plastic box, the size that might fit a deck or two of "Magic" type cards.*

KAYVAN: I can't get this open.

MR. SOBHANI: What is it?

The phone rings.

KAYVAN: The rings.

MR. SOBHANI: (*Into phone, overlapping.*) Hello? Alláh-u-abhá...

He goes to the kitchen, speaking in Persian. KAYVAN *follows.* CHRIS *appears at the DR door, dressed in an eclectic mix of African, Western and Persian styles.*

CHRIS: Chadwick! I thought you'd dropped off the face of the earth. Hey man, I came to see you in the hospital once or twice but you're always dozing.

CHAD *nods.*

CHRIS: Other than that, man, it's been bang-diddley-bang busy. I have more relatives now than I know what to do, surrounded by so much love!—So glad you're here, man.

CHAD: I have something for you.

CHRIS: Hey, you didn't need to do that!

CHAD: It's the Africa beads you gave me.

CHRIS: No, these were for you—

CHAD: My doctors said my treatment is working so…

CHRIS: That's great news.

CHRIS goes to give him a hug, CHAD is stiff. He holds out the beads.

CHAD: I don't need them anymore

CHRIS: Okay, I'll hold onto them.

MR. SOBHANI: There he is!

He and KAYVAN have reentered. MR. SOBHANI is trying to open Kayvan's box.

CHRIS: There they are!

The phone rings again.

MR. SOBHANI: This phone! (*Answering.*) Hello? Hold on please. (*To KAYVAN.*) Bring this to Nura.

KAYVAN: Okay. (*He exits into the DL bedroom.*)

MR. SOBHANI: (*To Chris.*) Maybe you can open this.

CHRIS: (*Trying to pry open the box.*) Magic cards! Excellent.

KAYVAN: (*Entering, in a loud whisper.*) She wants to know who it is.

MR. SOBHANI: It's a woman.

KAYVAN: Okay. (*He exits.*)

MR. SOBHANI: How are you, Mr. Chadwick? Sorry, things are very crazy.

CHAD: Fine, I was in the hospital.

MR. SOBHANI: Yes, we have been praying for you.

CHAD: Thanks.

CHRIS: (*Shaking box.*) These aren't cards in here, it's something hard.

He hands the box back to MR. SOBHANI. KAYVAN *has reentered.* MELINDA *enters from bathroom.*

MR. SOBHANI: (*To* KAYVAN.) Do you need to play this now, Kayvan?

MELINDA: Sirus, thank you for the room. Hi Chad.

CHRIS: Hi Mom!

MELINDA: Wow, don't you look… unique. I want a moment with you and Tahirih before we go out.

CHRIS: Hey, I'm going to present my new painting in a minute, no—thirty seconds!

CHRIS *exits.* MELINDA *follows him into the DR room. The phone rings offstage.*

MR. SOBHANI: (*To* KAYVAN, *indicating box.*) For now, put this away—did you find the rings?

KAYVAN: The rings are in there.

MR. SOBHANI: Eh?!

KAYVAN: Semowa told me to make it personal so I put them in this box.

MR. SOBHANI: Your box is so personal it has stolen the wedding rings.

NURA *enters from DL door with the phone.*

NURA: Bábá, phone.

KAYVAN: (*Sitting on the couch with* CHAD.) I'm such a big fat dope.

CHAD *looks at him.*

MR. SOBHANI: (*To phone.*) Hello? (*To* KAYVAN.) Go get a screwdriver!

KAYVAN *exits into UR door quickly.* NURA *comes down to look out the window at the wedding guests.*

NURA: How are you, Chad?

CHAD *exits into the bathroom.* MELINDA *enters from DR room.*

MELINDA: How's the bride?

NURA: Almost there—how are you?

MELINDA: A little nervous about going out there.

NURA: Yes. (*Begins to cross back towards the DL room.*)

MELINDA: I mean, we're not divorced, but people look at you as if it's all over.

NURA *stops and hugs* MELINDA.

NURA: No tears—we're going to go show we're okay. We're going to smile, have a good time, and they will see we're fine.

MELINDA: It's three months for you now?

NURA: Tahirih thinks he may try to use today to come back, but I don't think so.

MRS. SOBHANI: (*Entering.*) Hellooooo.

MELINDA: Parvin, let's see your nails.

MRS. SOBHANI *clicks her tongue and hides her hands.*

MELINDA: What happened? We made them up so nice last night!

MRS. SOBHANI: I cannot keep—I feel Bahá'u'lláh is mad at me.

MELINDA: Oh Jeez!

CHRIS *comes in with a large painting canvas, covered by a cloth. He sets it up on an easel in the middle of the room facing upstage.*

CHRIS: Mom, Mámán! Let's get everyone together. Where's Kayvan? (*He goes out front door.*)

MELINDA: (*Exiting UR.*) Be right back.

MRS. SOBHANI *has led* NURA *downstage to point out the window.*

MRS. SOBHANI: Únjá, dar-e-chádor   اونجا، در چادر نگه داشته.
negah dáshte.

[Trans: *Right there, holding the tent door open.*]

NURA: (*Seeing.*) Ámad.   آمد.

[Trans: *He came.*]

KAYVAN: (*Entering from UR door.*) Can't find the screwdriver!

MRS. SOBHANI: Chí míkháhí?   چی میخواهی؟

ACT 2, SCENE 3

[*Trans: What do you want?*]

MR. SOBHANI: (*At kitchen door, still on phone.*) Kayvan, come here please.

CHRIS: (*Entering.*) Okay everyone!

NURA *exits through UL door.* MRS. SOBHANI *and* KAYVAN *go into kitchen with* MR. SOBHANI.

CHRIS: They all just took off. (*He knocks on DL door.*) Tahirih, come out and see my painting!

TAHIRIH: (*Off.*) Not quite ready!

CHRIS: Come out anyway! That will draw the rest, like flies to honey.

The door opens and CHRIS *sees* TAHIRIH *before the audience does. He appears speechless a moment, then:*

CHRIS: Too much beauty. Must end life.

He mocks slitting his throat, falls to the ground, dies. She appears, most of the way to her bridal peak.

TAHIRIH: You planned that one. (*She scratches at an itchy stocking.*)

CHRIS: (*Raised from the dead.*) But did you get it—the whole Tahirih-unveiled, guy-slitting-throat thing?

TAHIRIH: Yeah. Hi, Chad.

CHAD: (*Having reentered.*) Oh, hi. You look…

TAHIRIH: (*Seeing flowers.*) Thank you.

CHAD: …great.

TAHIRIH: You didn't bring these, did you?

MELINDA: (*Reentering.*) Aren't they beautiful? What am I saying—Look at you!

CHRIS: I don't see a card.

TAHIRIH: Anyone gives flowers that big wants something.

CHRIS: Maybe they want to show their love—as do I! Everyone gather around, where's Hal? Kayvan, run and get Hal, be back in 12 seconds.

KAYVAN *runs out.* MR. *and* MRS. SOBHANI *are aside, speaking quietly.*

CHRIS: Mámán, Bábá... if you would—

MRS. SOBHANI: What is this box?

MR. SOBHANI: Nothing. (*He walks over and hands it to* CHAD *with a wink.*) See if you can open.

CHAD: Okay.

CHRIS: Chad, you want to come see?

CHAD *stays put, focuses on box. People gather around painting, try to show enthusiasm.* HAL *enters with* KAYVAN.

TAHIRIH: Let's see it.

CHRIS: This is my gift to all of you.

With a swoop of fabric, the painting is revealed.

ENSEMBLE: Oh!

The initial impressions are very good.

TAHIRIH: It's us!

KAYVAN: My hair is awesome!

MRS. SOBHANI: Very nice

MR. SOBHANI: Yes.

MELINDA: I love the outfits. Very African.

CHRIS: You recognize what you're wearing?

TAHIRIH: That's the cloth you brought back.

MELINDA: Oh yeah—see, it looks good on me!

CHRIS: Abstract expressionism didn't seem to speak to all of you, so I'm trying out a new thing: African expressionism.

TAHIRIH: Aren't we all a little dark?

CHRIS: Think of it as soulful. I tried to paint you all as if there were a little of myself in you.

HAL: That's right, we all kinda look like you.

MELINDA: (*To* CHRIS.) Maybe now would be a good time for me to give you my little speech.

KAYVAN: Look at Rustam, he looks like an ape! (*Laughs.*)

ACT 2, SCENE 3

TAHIRIH: That's okay, we're going to have to paint over him.

CHRIS *turns to her.*

TAHIRIH: Now that he's no longer around.

HAL: He's here.

TAHIRIH: You're kidding.

HAL: No. He said he's been in California the past few months. (*To* SOBHANIS.) Chris returned the gun, right? We didn't need it after all—the squirrel did himself in, chewed on the wrong wire.

MELINDA: The house?

HAL: It's fine—wish I could say the same for the squirrel.

CHRIS: We named him Bob—short for kabob.

TAHIRIH: Excuse me, Hal, where is he now?

HAL: Rustam? I told him to come in and walk out with us.

Silence.

HAL: Was that a bad idea?

The doorbell sounds. The door opens, everyone turns to see RUSTAM *enter.*

RUSTAM: Hello, happy to see me? You got my flowers—Hey, little sister, looking good!

TAHIRIH: (*To* CHRIS.) I'm not walking out there if he is with us.

RUSTAM: Are you still upset because our little misunderstanding?

CHRIS: I don't understand.

TAHIRIH: You better get him out of here or this wedding is canceled. (*She leaves.*)

RUSTAM: Must be too happy to have me back.

MR. SOBHANI: Let me check. (*He goes into the room.*)

RUSTAM: Where is my wife and my daughter? (*He goes to the UL door, but it's locked.*) Honey, you don't know how much I missed you two! (*Sees painting.*) Is that me? (*He laughs.*) Let me guess, she told you draw me like that.

CHRIS: She hasn't told me anything about you.

RUSTAM: Because nothing is to say. Chris, you and I—we are family now, so you don't mind if I tell you the truth about your painting. It doesn't move me, but you don't want to hear this now—Fast forward to the end of this night is what you're thinking, right? So go tell the princess whatever is her problem she should let go. We are Bahá'ís and we must forgive.

MR. SOBHANI *reenters, eerily calm. He motions* RUSTAM *to come to him.*

RUSTAM: Bábá-ján, did you talk some sense into her?

MR. SOBHANI: (*Quietly.*) It's good that you leave.

RUSTAM: She's just emotional—

MR. SOBHANI: It's 2 o'clock. In three, maybe four hours the wedding will be done—you make sure you are no longer in Florida.

RUSTAM: What ever she told you, she's lying!

MR. SOBHANI: I do find you and I do drag you to police.

Everyone is looking.

RUSTAM: Because why? Tell the nice people.

MR. SOBHANI: Because you are a thief! And my house is full with most precious things.

RUSTAM: Okay, but some of those things are mine. Nura, we take the baby and we go!

NURA *has entered with two large suitcases.*

MRS. SOBHANI: Nura! Kojá mírí?! نورا، کجا میری؟!

[*Trans: Where are you going?*]

RUSTAM: That's right, I take what is mine.

NURA: Here are all things you left.

RUSTAM: You forgot some… (*He moves to bedroom.*)

NURA: They are not there.

RUSTAM: What?

NURA: Your big man guns. I sold them. The money is now in your daughter's college fund.

RUSTAM: Very funny.

ACT 2, SCENE 3

NURA: Take your ring. (*She holds out her ring to him.*)

RUSTAM: Don't play games, we're leaving!

He takes her by the arm. All the other men come forward a step or two. He lets her go, gives everyone a look, then smiles. He takes the ring.

RUSTAM: Why so serious? This is a wedding—Remember how they whispered to you of love and then tore your heart!

He throws the ring in the air carelessly and leaves. NURA *goes to the window to watch.*

NURA: He's crying.

MRS. SOBHANI: Mídúne dárí negá-sh míkoní. میدونه داری نگاهش می‌کنی.

[*Trans: He knows you're watching.*]

MRS. SOBHANI *comes over and closes the blind.*

MR. SOBHANI: I am sorry, friends, for you had to see that, but seems it is God's will. (*To* CHRIS.) Why don't you get your bride?

CHRIS: So is someone going to explain what that was all about?

MRS. SOBHANI: Tahirih she understand.

CHRIS: Sure, but I don't get what harm having him at the wedding would do.

MRS. SOBHANI: (*Tapping his chest with her hand.*) Trust! Sometime, thing hold together marriage is only trust.

CHRIS: (*Touched.*) Okay.

KAYVAN: (*At painting.*) Hey Semowa, who is this guy in the corner here—all bent over?

CHRIS: That's my father. (*Knocks at DL door.*) He's gone, Tahirih!

HAL: Oh Jeez! (*He comes down to* CHRIS, *with an envelope he's taken from his pocket.*) Chris, I forgot— there's a letter for you.

TAHIRIH *opens the door.*

CHRIS: (*To* TAHIRIH.) Are you ready?

TAHIRIH: Are you?

HAL: Sorry, this came in the mail this morning.

TAHIRIH: What is it?

HAL: It's from Botswana.

CHRIS: I'll read it later—our guests are waiting.

TAHIRIH: Open it, I could use a minute.

   CHRIS *opens it, and the two look at the letter together.*

CHAD: Oh, I did it.

   All this time, CHAD *has been working on opening the box. He took a penny from his pocket, and trying it, the box popped right open.*

CHAD: I got the box open.

MR. SOBHANI: Kayvan, look!

   KAYVAN *and* MR. SOBHANI *come down to join* CHAD. MRS. SOBHANI *comforts* NURA *by the window.* HAL *has returned to be beside* MELINDA *at the painting.*

MR. SOBHANI: How you did?!

CHAD: I used a penny.

MR. SOBHANI: (*Patting* CHAD *on the back.*) He turns copper to gold!

CHAD: It's M-M-M-Magiiiiiic.

KAYVAN: Chad saved the day!

CHAD: Yeah I did.

TAHIRIH: What are you shouting about?

KAYVAN: Chad—

MR. SOBHANI: (*Silencing him.*) Tchup.

KAYVAN: It's a secret, and you have to trust us!

   KAYVAN *almost closes the box again, but* MR. SOBHANI *prevents him.*

MR. SOBHANI: Easy!

TAHIRIH: Whatever. (*She goes back to reading the letter.*)

MR. SOBHANI: (*To* KAYVAN.) Put this in your pocket and don't close!

HAL: (*To* MELINDA.) I fixed the front door… found a job too, teaching test prep part time.

ACT 2, SCENE 3

MELINDA: Chris told me. I thought we could sit together.

HAL: That'd be great.

MELINDA: We're still married, right?

HAL: Of course.

They move further downstage where MR. SOBHANI *is holding up Chad's penny.*

MR. SOBHANI: A Bahá'í, he looks at himself, he says, I am copper. But by aid of God, I become gold. (*He takes off his own ring and holds it up to compare with the penny.*) A Bahá'í, he looks at others, he says, I see only gold. (*Putting penny in his own hand.*) Me. Copper! Pfthh!

CHAD: Not worth much.

MR. SOBHANI: But you… I see only gold. (*He puts the ring in* CHAD's *hand.*)

CHAD: Why?

MR. SOBHANI: Because that is the way Bahá'u'lláh sees you. He sees you, Chadwick, as pure gold.

CHAD: Wow.

MR. SOBHANI: Now it is time. You will walk with us, Chadwick.

CHAD: (*Handing* MR. SOBHANI *the ring.*) Here you go.

MR. SOBHANI: That is for you.

CHAD: Your wedding ring?

MR. SOBHANI: When you are through with hospital and doctors, you give back to me. I keep your penny.

CHAD: But what about your wife?

MR. SOBHANI: She still will be my wife, with ring or without. You cannot get out that easy. (*He laughs.*) It's time!

TAHIRIH: Dad, wait—we want you all to hear this letter from Chris's father.

The group comes together around the couch.

CHRIS: (*Reading.*) "Thank you for your invitation. I am sorry I cannot come to see with my own eyes my son's happiness. I wish you—above all—happiness. In Africa, when a man and a woman marry, the people are all happy. Please God, you are all happy, and sheltered from all pain. The Baháʼís must be truly happy! Unlike the man who drinks alcohol to forget his fight with his neighbor, the Baháʼí cannot drink. Unlike the man who sleeps with the young virgin, you cannot lose your pain through sex. Unlike the man who leaves his wife in one village when she's angry to go to his other wife in the next village, you cannot leave your pain behind you. I once tried to leave my pain behind me, but my pain only grew. I gave up the Baháʼí Faith because the Baháʼís disappointed me because there was pain in their house. And so I chose to bury my bones in a small house near where I was born. And I tried every way I could to lose my pain but all I lost was time. And then when my time seemed up, I looked up, and an angel had come down from heaven and knocked me on the head and said WAKE UP! You are still somebody... because you are not forgotten, because Baháʼuʼlláh has not forgotten you. The boy was His messenger. Through the mysterious working of His law I was remembered. And the boy when I saw him, I was angry because I had nothing and he had everything and I am sorry what I've done to you. But despite my anger, he responded with love. I saw that—that was real, and he did not fake that. And then I knew, I knew what He had done for this young man, and that this house so full of pain also had the remedy like no other house around. This house is full of pain but this house has the remedy. So use it, my Baháʼí brothers and sisters, my Baháʼí son and daughter, use it and bring happiness to the world. On this day, may your gathering shine bright with the light of love and happiness and bring healing to this world of ours, which is waiting, which is waiting...

A moment of silence.

CHRIS: Mom, you had something you wanted to say?

MELINDA, *now flooded with emotion, shakes her head.*

TAHIRIH: Daddy, open the blinds. Let us see them all.

MR. SOBHANI *moves downstage and gestures as if opening blinds. As he does so, the lights come up over the audience.*

CHRIS: Who imagined it could be so beautiful?

MR. SOBHANI: So many marriages.

MRS. SOBHANI: So many hopes.

NURA: No guarantees.

CHRIS: Shall we?

TAHIRIH: Let's do it.

KAYVAN: It's going to be hot.

CHAD: Shining like gold.

HAL: Out of the pan

MELINDA: And into the fire.

The actors step forward and take their curtain call.

End of Play

ON THE ROOFTOP WITH BILL SEARS

A one man play based on the life and writings
of Mr. William Sears (1911-1992)

To Mr. Sears,
and
to my Grandfather,
James Bowen

Setting

WCAU-TV Studios in Philadelphia, USA. May 1953.

Cast

BILL SEARS   He's 42 and charismatic, with a strong mixture of both humor and melancholy. A natural performer and storyteller, he now finds himself alone, wrestling with a dilemma that reaches into his core, striving to retrieve the honest answer.

This script represents the original vision of the play as was first staged in April 2004, performed by Mark Perry with direction by J. Chachula. When the play began touring, adjustments were made to reflect the need for minimal props and set. Along with these changes, a less realistic approach to the premise of the play was adopted. Whereas this script clearly sets the play in Philadelphia in 1953, the touring production made it feel like Bill Sears, a spirit living outside of time, stumbles upon this place and this memory, and he decides to spend some time with us and to relive this crucial moment of his life. That being said, the spoken dialogue changed very little.

ON THE ROOFTOP WITH BILL SEARS

The set is a 1950s TV studio, which is actually a converted radio studio. This is one of seven such studios at WCAU-TV in downtown Philadelphia. The studio is dimly lit at first with some light on stage right, where we see the set of a park scene. There is a tree and a bench covered by a cloth. On a chalkboard is written the title, "In the Park with Bill Sears." At stage left, apart from the set and still in darkness, there is a make-shift dressing area with a mirror. A kitchen area is offstage left. A sound room is upstage. Still portraits of WCAU personalities hang on the wall along with other items. BILL *appears at the door. He is a middle-aged man, made up to look like an old man. He speaks to someone offstage.*

BILL: Good show today, Paul. No, go ahead, I'll get the lights.

    BILL *comes in, full of snap. He wears striped pants, a flat gray coat, a light checkered vest, and a string tie. He stops.*

BILL: I love that hush, the quiet of a dark theater… or a TV or radio studio, as the case may be. It's a silence that vibrates with anticipation, every atom poised to bring into being whatever one might fancy. You could say, let's go back to the Renaissance, to Spain, to Seville… or to Rome of the 1st Century, or east to the Orient and points yet unknown. You could call up stories of people long gone. You could bring a man back from the dead. Yes! You can bring a man back from the dead, let him live again, let something of his essence mingle in our midst for a while, so you might enjoy his company, gain from his experience. All you have to do is ask, and this hush—this pure soil for the cultivation of the soul—it responds. And for a span of time, you can forget that it's 1953 and that you're in Philadelphia.

He turns on the lights.

BILL: You remember that joke. "I entered a contest once. First prize was a week in Philadelphia. Second prize: two weeks in Philadelphia." WCAU, a 7-studio house broadcasting radio and television. I do a daily show, plus my sports gig (*he waves an Eagles pennant*) and then there's "In the Park." Some Sundays, I like to take a little extra time after the show, to reflect. I don't have much quiet time at home between my two sons' escapades and the menagerie of pets and guests my wife Marguerite keeps. Let's see what we got on.

He turns on a speaker monitor and we hear music.

BILL: Ah, Guy Lombardo. Must be Stu in the booth—he loves the old sugar-stick.

He turns down the music, when he discovers a cup of coffee and a donut by his dressing table. There's an envelope next to them.

BILL: Oh, isn't that nice? Coffee with cream and (*sniffs*) two sugars. And a honey-glazed. Heaven. And a letter. (*He picks it up and sniffs it.*) It's a contract. (*He shakes it next to his ear.*) To renew the show for another year. Boss shows me into his office the other day: "Sears, Television is big, very big, and it's getting bigger.

The CBS people, they're happy, very happy with your show. Stick with us, Bill, and you'll be a star." And now they're offering me... (*Listens carefully to letter.*) Forty-five? No. (*He weighs it in his hands.*) Fifty! $50,000. (*He sighs.*) Sounds... delicious. Just one problem.

The number '16' is written prominently on his dressing mirror. He wipes it away and writes '17' in its place.

BILL: I'm calling it "The Divine Dilemma." And today is Day 17. (*Talking to God.*) Only 2 days left. Beyond that, my conscience is clean. (*To audience.*) How do I put this...? I have a friend—works here at WCAU—who suspects that Jesus Christ has returned, and is wondering what to do about it. The answer is obvious, right? Christ hasn't returned, because when He comes, everyone is going to know it. That's how we know He's come: all the noise, the fire with the angels singing, horns blowing. Right. (*He shakes his head as if he's in complete agreement with that.*) Still... my friend suspects it anyway, and claims to have some proof. Good proof. Great proof... except for the angels, the horns and the universal cataclysm. What would you do? Really, given that point of view, what would you advise? Should my friend give up a good livelihood and fame to go and share this message? Because no one knows about it. Just like the first time He came—my friend says—when only twelve believed in Him, and He sent them out into the world saying, go out and share the Gospel with all nations.

My friend really loves his job. Don't get me wrong, the industry has its dark side, its temptations. (*He picks up a record.*) This record arrived the other day addressed to me... (*He flips it around — a $20 bill is taped to the back of the sleeve*) with a 20 spot taped to the sleeve. Might be a good record, it'll certainly get a lot of airplay.

He pulls off the $20 bill and tapes it in a prominent spot.

BILL: But I say treat people fairly and honestly, and for the most part, they'll do well by you. Take a guy like Ed Sullivan. He's got a reputation to be the "great stone face," but I've found he's one of the genuinely nice people in the business. He's invited us on his show twice now, and because of that, this new rag, TV Guide, did a feature on us. So all in all, things are looking up for the show, for me.

I hope you won't think this immodest. Praise doesn't mean that much to me. My priorities are clear: First, air. Second, water. Third... I dunno, food? Well, praise is after air and water, definitely. Thank you for laughing. So it's not just the money. (*He picks up the envelope.*) Besides, 50,000 isn't what it used to be, say, in 1912, when you could get a beer for a nickel. Still... Wanna see what I do for such a sum?

He throws a sheet off the park bench to reveal several stuffed animal puppets.

BILL: I talk to the animals! I play dress up and take pleasure in the fact that when I'm finished putting on the makeup and costume, I look like my grandfather! I mean it's all good and fine to play make-believe every once in a while, to have fun, but to be paid a salary that a doctor—someone who saves human lives on a regular basis—doesn't make. Dear God, where will it all end—did you ever catch yourself mid-sentence and wonder who is this speaking with my mouth because it sounds frighteningly like my father?!

    My father. Money meant so much to my father. And he wouldn't see this kind of money in 20 years of hard work. Factory work. I look in the mirror some days and I don't see myself. I see him. Looking back at me, with a look of disbelief in his eyes. And we have this ongoing dialogue, he and I—actually the mirror and I—about whether what I do is actually worth anything.

He hides part of his face with his hands.

BILL: Maybe it's just the mustache.

He starts taking off his makeup.

BILL: So each Sunday, I'm transformed from my father into my grandfather then back to my father again. And the three of us enjoy a donut and a cup of coffee. So let's see, how do you split coffee and a donut three ways? See, if Christ had returned, He could do this. Or was that Moses? To Grandfather, the coffee. I'll hold the donut. And for Father…

He goes to the refrigerator and pulls out a bottle of beer. He blows the dust off it, but does not open it.

BILL: For father, Milwaukee tap water. He's Irish after all. (*Holding up the bottle as if toasting his father.*) That you may see no one but yourself in the mirror. On a Saturday night Father would stand for hours around the piano at Hennessy's House with the only other two Irishmen in town and they would sing one short song over and over. (*Sings.*)

"Ooooh… McGinty was dead and McCarthy didn't know it;
McCarthy was dead and McGinty didn't know it.
They both lay there dead in the very same bed
And neither didn't know that the other was dead."

The phone rings. He picks it up.

BILL: Bill Sears. Hi Stu. Sorry to hear that. Sure. Of course. Okay. (*He hangs up.*) That was the DJ who's on now, Stu, and he's got a stomach flu—

He hears his rhyme and thinks. He reaches for a pen and paper.

BILL: Just saying he may need me to cover for him.

The phone rings again.

BILL: Pete's Porcelain Palace… 30 seconds? No, I got it. Go do your thing.

He scribbles a few lines, and then goes into the sound room. He comes back out and grabs a horn (sound effect) that is hanging on the wall. Music comes up on P.A. system. When the song fades, the "On the Air" sign comes on. We hear BILL*'s voice.*

BILL: This is Bill Sears in Studio 7, and here's a limerick for you: I just got a call from Stu, seems he has a touch of the flu, said he couldn't sit, and if I could pinch hit, then he could take... (*the honk of a horn*) ...a trip to the loo. If you're listening, Marguerite, I'll be coming home soon.

We hear Benny Goodman's "Sing, Sing, Sing." BILL reenters.

BILL: Benny Goodman's 'Sing, Sing, Sing' is an ol' stand by for DJ's. At 8 ½ minutes, it gives us time to grab a snack and visit the little boy's room. Good thing I was here. Silence can be bad for a radioman's career. Now, where was I? I forget. So I'll do what any old codger would: I'll start at the beginning.

I was born in Duluth, Minnesota on March 28, 1911. Sometimes I wonder if Father never forgave me for missing Saint Patrick's Day by less than two weeks. I was born in a caul. Wrapped in a veil, my father said. My Uncle Duffy was more picturesque. "Jesus, Mary, and Joseph, and all the saints in purgatory! The laddie's come in a cocoon."

I began to walk when I was ten months old, but I began to speak when I was only six months. It made my father very nervous. Especially since the first word I said was not, "Daddy" but "God". Apparently, I heard it a lot around the house, generally followed by language less religious in character.

By the time I was a year-and-a-half old, my father was quite frightened of me. I knew several words that he didn't. It was at this time that I first had the dream. When I told Mother about my dream she told Father. He wanted to take me to a doctor, but Mother said, "He's just precocious."

"He's weird," Father told her.

All I could recall myself about the dream the first time I had it was that the room had been full of a wonderful bright light, that I was very happy, and that I wanted to remain there. September 20, 1912. Mother said she remembered the day of my dream very clearly. It was the morning that Father came downstairs after being desperately ill. He'd eaten some string beans from a bad jar and had been poisoned. For three days he thought he was going to die. At the height of his fever he confessed to Mother that ten years ago when they had first been married he'd taken Alma Jensen to a barn dance, and he didn't want to die with that on his conscience. Unfortunately for him, he recovered.

By the time I was five I was making my poor father's life a misery. I just had all these questions: Why was the sky blue? Where did a laugh go after you heard it? If the earth was round and people were walking on all sides of it, which side was up? Why was Sammy Agnew black and why was I white – most of the time? Did God have a wife? Where was His house? Could He speak Chippewa Indian like Uncle Walter? Did He really love everybody? Even old lady Yellow-jacket who chased us kids with her umbrella? Why did He make mosquitoes? And flies that could walk upside down on the ceiling? The big questions really unnerved my father. I seemed to have an inordinate interest in God, and he didn't care to discuss it with me.

One day at the circus, while the bare-back riders were galloping through the big rings of fire, I turned to Father and said suddenly, "Is that what hell is like?"

Father nearly swallowed his cigar. "Don't ask me, I've lived all my life in Minnesota."

"Where does *God* live, Father? How big is He? Does He have brown eyes?"

We left the tent immediately. Father stopped at a side-show and bought me a rubber ball. "Here," he said, "play ball. Be like the other little boys. Bounce the ball on the ground."

I did, obediently. Then I looked up at him proudly. "God made the ground."

About a month later, according to Mother, I had the dream a second time. I didn't say anything about it until my father came home from work.

"The man came again," I said.

"Who came?" Father laughed.

"The man."

"What man?"

"The man in light."

"Where?"

"In my dream again."

"Ethel! He's at it again."

Mother came hurrying in. "What's wrong?"

Father was already putting on his coat. "He's seen that man in a light in his dream again."

Mother picked me up tenderly and kissed me. "Of course, he has." She hugged me to her. "We all have nasty bad dreams."

"It was a good dream," I told her.

"What did the man look like?"

"I don't know."

"What did he say?"

"Don't follow in their footsteps."

The very next morning Father was shaving when I came into the bathroom.

"What's my name?" I asked him.

Father had often played this game with me. "Your name is William."

"Then why did he call me Peter?"

"Who?"

"The man in my dream last night."

Father cut his chin. "Ethel!"

Mother was very patient about it. "Are you sure he called you Peter, dear?"

I nodded. "He said: 'Fish like Peter.' "

Father went to work that morning with his face half shaved. "It's not normal. He talks like an old man. He'll be dead before he's six." Whenever my father became upset he talked with a brogue and waxed poetic. "If I'd known what was coming that dark March night, I'd have stuffed him back into the 'caul' and returned him."

They say there's an age when the child looks to its father, looks into his eyes, searching for unconditional acceptance. There's a window of time and if the child doesn't find it, that window closes, and the boy has to go elsewhere for that acceptance.

If we were on Television Playhouse, this is where our troubled protagonist would reach for the bottle of beer, BUT! I'm more interested in this donut here...

He bites the donut. The phone rings.

BILL: (*Answers.*) Bill Sears. Stu, you're back! How'd it work out? Oh, good. Did you catch my bit? No? Ask your mother when you get home. Okay, call if you need me. (*Looks around.*) I know where I am, I know where I am. Donut. Beer. Dad. Dream. Ah!

One night I had exactly the same dream again. Only this time I was old enough to remember it clearly. So I wrote it down, all about the beautiful shiny white figure that came to me and brought a peace and rapture such as words can never describe.

I decided that I'd better go and tell my grandfather about my dream. Grandfather didn't always know the answers, but he always let me ask questions. I found Grandfather inside his barn singing at the top of his lungs:

(*Sings.*) "You will eat, bye and bye,
In that glorious land above the sky;
Work and pray, live on hay,
There'll be pie in the sky when you die!"

I told him about my dream. I asked him if he'd ever seen anything like that. He said no, but he <u>wished</u> he had.

I asked him, "Why is it, Grandfather, that it's so easy to talk to you about God? Here I am a young boy and there you are an old man. We both like it but nobody else seems to want to. "Maybe it's because I am old and you're young. You're close to God on one end, and I'm close to Him on the other. In between, they don't care so much."

I once heard our neighbor Mrs. Casey say Grandfather would never see the inside of the pearly gates. I knew that if you missed church on Sunday it was a mortal sin and you were damned into hell fire forever. I figured it out. Grandfather had missed over three thousand times. I wasn't interested in going to heaven at all if Grandfather wasn't there.

One Sunday I skipped church and took a chance on eternal hellfire. I went with Grandfather in his buggy down by the Mississippi River. There'd been a bad storm, and all the people who lived along the flats had been flooded out. Grandfather was helping to rescue their things. We worked until very late in the afternoon. When we came back Grandfather got a tongue-lashing from Grandma, and I was sent upstairs to bed until Father came home to deal with me.

I knew right away that this wouldn't be a "man-to-man talk," or a light willow switch, this was a razor-strapper. Father swung his razor-strap as though he were chopping wood. What was even worse, was the way he walked up the stairs. His feet could play on stairs with more feeling than Mr. Tilley on the church organ on Sunday.

"Let's get it over with," he said.

"Yes, sir."

"This hurts me a lot worse than it does you."

"But not in the same place."

That got me a few extra strokes.

I went down to join Grandfather at the barn. He was sitting on the oats-box.

"Have a seat, son," he said.

I shook my head. "Not just yet."

Grandfather nodded sympathetically. "You're thinking that if you'd lied about where we'd been this afternoon you'd have a more comfortable seat on your breeches right now, right?"

I nodded.

Grandfather laughed. "Better to be miserable on the bottom end and proud of yourself on the top end," he told me. "That's character. Forget your rump. You did a good thing helping those people at the river."

Grandfather got me a soft cushion out of the buggy. I settled into it very carefully. I liked being with Grandfather. I liked the smell of his clothes, his wrinkled cheeks with those short, sharp whiskers that scratched when he hugged me.

Before I went home that night Grandfather told me, "Never stop asking questions." Then he made me promise, cross my heart and hope to die, that I wouldn't stop. "There must be something better somewhere than what we've got so far. Some day you'll find out what your dream means. I hope I'm around when you do. I've been looking for something myself, for all my years."

Inside the barn was a world that belonged only to me and Grandfather. That world inspired this show. And now in a way we're opening it up to all these other people. We changed it around a bit. Instead of a barn, we have a park. I play the old man. The boy became Albert the chipmunk. We added some other animal puppets like Sir Geoffrey the Giraffe and Magnolia the Ostrich here. And now every Sunday, at 12 noon, the animals and I are transformed into electromagnetic radiation and beamed abroad to CBS television stations all across this nation. I imagine it to be like Grandfather's barn stretching out over the whole country, and all are welcome, and no question will go... unspoken.

So maybe I can show you the kind of thing we do here. You see, the old man, whose name is Bill... Oh, put me in a dress and call me Mabel! I have managed to come to this point without properly introducing myself.

He offers to shake hands with an audience member.

BILL: Bill Sears. And the program is "In the Park with Bill Sears." Now this old man because of the purity of his heart can talk to the animals in the park where he goes every day. I don't have a particular script memorized. We don't actually memorize in TV. We use prompt cards!

He pulls out a magazine from his things.

BILL: Okay, I got it. Let me take a moment to get into character.

He puts on a hat, picks up a cane and assumes the character of the older man.

BILL: Hello, Albert. Hello, Sir Geoffrey. Hello, Magnolia.

(*Mimicking Albert's voice:*) "What are you reading, Bill?"

(*Older man again:*) This, my dear friend, is a recent issue of my favorite magazine, which I discovered the other night by my bedside. Now, Albert, finding it there struck me as very strange as my wife and I had very recently agreed not to subscribe to this magazine. And yet there it was! (*Breaking character.*) This bit is more or less true, but we'll come to that soon enough.

He listens as if the giraffe (Sir Geoffrey) is asking him something.

BILL: Why, Sir Geoffrey, I imagine it was my Marguerite who put it there. All of you remember my wife Marguerite? Eyes the color of robins' eggs?

(*Mimicking Magnolia's voice:*) "Ostrich eggs are a much nicer color!"

(*Older man again:*) I'm sure that ostrich eggs are a very nice color as well, Magnolia.

He listens as if the chipmunk (Albert) is asking him something.

BILL: Well, Albert, there's a very interesting thing about this particular magazine. Just listen to these headlines.

"LOST CONTINENT OF ATLANTIS DISCOVERED OFF COAST OF PORTUGAL"

"SHAKESPEARE REALLY BACON"

"MARTIANS LAND IN NEW JERSEY"

He looks over at Albert the chipmunk.

BILL: Now, you don't need to be so nervous, Albert, these headlines aren't actually true.

All the animals ask, "they're not?"

BILL: No!

(*Mimicking Sir Geoffrey's voice:*) "So what kind of magazine prints untrue headlines?"

(*Older man again:*) Believe it or not, this is a good, reputable magazine. They're not saying these headlines are true—quite the opposite in fact. This magazine asked newspaper editors around the nation to submit some *imaginary* headlines that the editor felt would arouse the greatest excitement.

"NO MORE WINTER EVER"

I like the sound of that one too! But there was ONE headline these hard-boiled newspapermen agreed would be the most electrifying of all. Do you want to guess what it was? Magnolia.

(*Mimicking Magnolia's voice:*) "Birds proved smarter than people."

(*Older man again:*) Hmm, that would give a whole new ring to being called a "bird brain," wouldn't it? Sir Geoffrey, you have one?

(*Mimicking Sir Geoffrey's voice:*) "Long neck a sign of superior intelligence."

(*Older man again:*) Well, it certainly signals a nearness to God, doesn't it? Albert, you have one?

He leans down as if Albert is whispering to him.

BILL: "Enough nuts harvested to feed entire planet." Wow, those would all make wonderful headlines, but the number one headline consisted of only two words.

He gets up, walks to the chalkboard and writes.

BILL: CHRIST RETURNS.

He takes off his hat and puts off the character of the old man, and gives a significant look to the audience.

BILL: A journalist would give anything to be the one to break that story. My friend—the one who believes Christ has returned—he's in broadcasting. So what does he do? Does he try to break the story? (*Imitating news telegraph*) Dee-de-dee-dee. News Flash! We interrupt this regularly scheduled program to bring you the following news bulletin: Long awaited Messiah, Jesus Christ, finally returns! Citizens of Philadelphia wonder what took so long… No, of course not! The other day he walks into his boss' office tells him he's thinking about resigning. His boss gets agitated. They're very attached to him, you see. (*Mimicking his boss:*) "Now, now, if you leave, and we have to break the contract with the sponsor, 56 people are going to lose their jobs. That's 56 families with no food on the table." Just to add another wrinkle to his dilemma.

A beat.

BILL: So I'm ten, eleven years old, and still I didn't know what my dream meant. I took Grandfather's advice and started to read the Bible.

Bill pulls out a copy of the Bible. He sits and starts to flip through it, quickly displaying a lack of interest.

BILL: I found it very difficult and was just about to give up in favor of "Nick Carter, Master Detective," when I was told that no one was encouraged to read the Bible for himself. From that moment on, it became a "must".

I kept skipping through the chapters looking for the shiny white man in my dream. Father didn't want me becoming a religious fanatic, so whenever he saw me reading the Bible he'd take it away from me. He hid our two copies, so I borrowed one from Saphead Phillips.

That was the beginning of the great religious feud between me and Father. I tried reading in bed. "Time to sleep, son" and he'd turn off the light. I would tiptoe out of bed: "Time to read, Father" and click on the light again. One night he saw the light through my keyhole. "William!!" So I began to hang a blanket over the door so that the light wouldn't shine through the keyhole or cracks. That lasted four nights. I even tried disguising the Bible as my math book. Some days you know you'd just like to go up on the roof where no one pays you any mind. Read what you want to read. Believe what you want to believe.

One day, while I was cleaning the attic (this was part of my punishment for the math book scheme), I figured out that I could run a long extension cord with a socket on it right down into my bedroom from the attic. I wasn't taking any chance on this light being discovered, so I ran the cord along the pipes, down the wall, and took it right into bed with me. Mother thought I'd reformed. I heard her tell Father, "Something wonderful has happened. William is making his own bed each day."

At night I would make a nice little tent out of the bed-covers, then take the electric light right under the sheets and blankets. Inside my teepee I could read to my heart's content. One night, I dipped into the New Testament, and the first words that hit my eye were:

"...and his face did shine as the sun,

and his raiment was white as the light."

It was my shiny man! I let out a yell, straightened up in bed, and jerked the extension cord so hard it caused a short circuit and burned out every light in the house.

I hid the cord and went out into the hall to help Father, who was trying to find out what on earth could have happened. I could hardly wait until the next night to get back to my reading. I pored over the words. The more I read, the more certain I was that what I'd seen in my dream was the Messiah. It was Christ. He'd returned and was waiting for me somewhere. I was positive when I read the words:

> "I go away but return again."
>
> "You shall see the Son of Man coming in the glory of the Father."
>
> "When He, the Spirit of Truth, is come, He will lead you to all Truth."

For a whole week, I kept searching through the Bible for more about the shiny white figure. Then came the night of the big explosion. I had just turned back to David and Goliath. It was a great fight, and I was so worried about David missing Goliath with the sling-shot that I didn't hear Father slip quietly into the room and approach the edge of the bed, wondering what the funny glow was coming from beneath the blankets. He slowly lifted one end of the blanket and peered in at me. David was just getting ready to let fly at the giant Goliath. Naturally, I didn't know it was Father's face. His eyes looked so fierce I thought it was Goliath. I threw the book in the air, screamed at the same time, and like David I fired my sling-shot. I swung the extension cord and hit Father right between the eyes with a sixty-watt bulb. It made a very loud explosion. Father shouted, grabbed for me, held on to the bedclothes, and pulled them on top of himself as he fell to the floor.

My sister Ella was first on the scene. She began dancing round in the doorway hysterically. "He's shot him! He's shot him! Father's shot William dead!"

Mother turned the bedroom light on and saw me cringing against the wall on the far side of the bed. Father was still trying to fight his way out of the blankets. When Mother uncovered Father, he began to crawl across the floor towards me, accusing me of deliberately trying to blind him.

"I thought you were Goliath," I said.

His eyes looked like the cyclops'. Mother cooled him down, and she and Ella helped him to pick the glass fragments out of his hair and eyebrows.

"I just wanted to learn what was in the Bible."

"Then go and ask Father Hogan," Father shouted. "That's what I pay my pew-rent for. Let him earn the money."

I told him, "Someday I'm going to find out what my dream means, and I'm going to go all over the world and tell people about God."

And you know what? My father never tried to discourage me from that. It made him nervous and he didn't like to talk about it, but he never said I was being foolish. When Father was young he was going to be a great actor. He was going to sacrifice everything for it. Everybody had discouraged him, but he said he felt deep down inside that it was the only thing in the world he really wanted to do. Father never got to be a famous actor. He met mother instead.

Earn the money. Like he said about father Hogan, let him earn the money! It was like Father's soul had been split in two by this obsession with earning money. And yet this (*indicating the studio*) was all he wanted to do. Acting. This is my father's dream. I'm living my father's dream.

He unconsciously opens the bottle of beer.

BILL: Oh. That was strange.

He puts the beer down and away from him.

BILL: That isn't even mine. I haven't touched alcohol in years.

He picks up the bottle, reads its label.

BILL: "The champagne of beers." I'm reminded of a poem.

> (*Reciting.*) Gone are the days we all held dear,
> The bar, the sawdust, and five-cent beer.
> Dimly remembered, how quickly he passes,
> That white-aproned bar-keep, his bottles and glasses.
>
> Gone are the doors that swung both ways,
> Gone are the memories of free-lunch days.

> How different the times of now from then—
> A toast to the days when men were men!

I was in grade school when I wrote it. Inspiration descended as I was sitting in a barber's chair listening to some old men reminisce. It was published… (*Nods his head.*) in Captain Billy's *Whiz Bang* magazine, and I received a royalty check for seven dollars and fifty cents. It was great to be a writer. I remember wondering if beer tasted anything like strawberry soda.

He sniffs the bottle, then puts it down.

BILL: So father moved the family from Minnesota to where he could find work. Guess where. I'll give you a hint.

He turns beer bottle so a particular part of the label faces the audience.

BILL: Milwaukee! Right, Milwaukee, wow! It had lights downtown that went off and on. Grandfather had warned me about the big city. "It's not like the country. Don't forget the things I've been telling you." And you know, he was right! It was new and exciting and full of so many things that in a year I forgot nearly everything he'd told me.

But I learned some things too. I learned that dreams have a way of not coming true. I learned that, in fact, sometimes you wake up from your dream and realize your house is being robbed. I had just started university when the Great Depression began. So I hurried home to help the family starve. For more than two years I never had more than twenty-five cents in cash in my pocket. I never saw a movie, never rode in a street-car or bus, never ate an ice-cream cone or drank a soda. I began to read the Bible again, but only because we couldn't afford a newspaper.

A thought strikes him. He starts moving around pieces of furniture and scenery, trying to depict what he is describing.

BILL: There's this image I have stuck in my head. A figure on the rooftop, silhouetted in moonlight, arms outstretched, and waiting... You see, I wasn't the only fool who dreamed that Christ would return. Oh, no, this was a reverie that many a believer has been caught up in. Remember the Great Disappointment from history class? Long before the Depression. 1844. That was the year He was supposed to come back.

He gestures towards the "Christ returns" on the chalkboard.

BILL: All the signs were there; the prophecies seemed to line right up. A guy named... Miller—William Miller—Upstate New York, late 1820s, discovers that the 2300-day prophecy in Daniel 8 is about to run out. Jesus was about to return. He was convinced. So what do you do? The end of the world is coming and people are going around worrying about—I don't know—hair pins and wagon wheels. So Miller did what we would probably do—he kept it pretty much to himself. He was no preacher! But his conscience plagued him. Finally he broke down and begged God for help: If you want me to share this teaching, show me a sign. Within half an hour, his nephew shows up and says, Uncle, our church wants you to preach next Sunday on the Second

Coming. Understandably he was... Furious! But he preached anyway. Before long, one in seventeen Americans becomes a Millerite.

1844 comes, and they work out a particular month and day. That night arrives. We're out there on the roof of a house we've just signed the deed over to our more skeptical relations who are inside. But no need for such possessions in the land of bliss. Wearing our Sunday best, we climb out the window onto the roof. We stand up there, calling out: "Jesus! Jesus! Take me now, Jesus! I'm ready for you!" and so on through the night on the roof with the waves of faith coming and going.

We feel at one moment that through the concentrated power of our faith that we alone can cause the moon to turn to blood and the stars to fall from heaven. He said with the faith of a mustard seed we could cause the mountain to move but with the flourishing tree of faith firmly rooted in our hearts we feel at that moment that this, the moon is about to break in two and the stars will fall and that our Lord will emerge resplendent, glorious, and dismissive of our skeptical relations inside playing cards. Concentrating. The moon about to break... to break. Break! BREAK!

The silence from heaven was deafening. "Jesus? The world of the faithful awaits you! We stand here trying to keep our balance, to keep from falling. The roof is pitched, Jesus—"

How long can we stay on the rooftop? How long before we have to swallow our certitude and go back inside. Our skeptical relations inside the house smile and try hard not to gloat. A part of them was up on the roof too.

He never came. Almost 2000 years we've waited. No Judgment. No fire. No Paradise descending. The world was awaiting its Promised One, to make it whole again. No dice. I think this is the greatest headline because it is our greatest disappointment. Of course, they'll say, you have to have faith. No man knows the hour. It comes down to trust. Trust in the son, trust in the Father. I don't know if you've noticed. I don't have a lot of trust in my father.

Oh, Depression. It's not as if my dream were that important in the vast scheme of human disappointment. I'd probably interpreted it wrong, and it had nothing to do with the Second Coming. It was just a comforting presence. A self remedy for poor parenting.

Grandfather wrote to me: "Quit worrying about the Depression. Write about it. It'll make a lot better poem than "the bar, the sawdust, and five cent beer." I took his advice, but instead of a poem, I wrote my first play. It won an award. They sent me a plaque. Father hung it on the wall. "It's a fine thing, son. What a pity you can't eat it."

Playwriting, playwriting. Please tell any poor soul bewitched by the Siren of playwriting to run in the other direction. It took me nine plays—NINE PLAYS—to realize: Theatre is as miserly a master as it is beautiful a mistress. So I became a radio announcer and hopped around the country from job to job. At a certain point, my dream just faded. No one talked about it. Father was no longer nervous when I talked with him, because I never mentioned God any more. To me, it seemed a pity. I had lost an inward glow, a sense of purpose. I was an average, unhappy, unfulfilled human being like everyone else; get up, go to work, go to bed, die.

I mean, sure, it's great to be on the radio, and now TV. People know you, they respect you – eventually they even start to pay you, but what is this? We're selling ourselves, posing for pictures all confidence but really deep down, aren't we just groveling, craving attention, paranoid about money, squirreling away nuts for these piddley little controlled lives? We're really just pleading the Universe, don't hurt me, don't hurt me. Don't break my little fragile bubble of a life. But is this reality? I'm staring Life in the face and it's looking back at me with hollow eyes. Life should not have hollow eyes. But is that life? Or is it a mirror, and they're my eyes? My eyes should not be hollow. I've known something better. Long ago, maybe, but there was something there. Something basic to our experience – something meaningful, something beautiful. I tell you I never felt so lost in my life. And I was looking for a way out.

And that's when I met Marguerite. I felt as though someone had just turned on all the lights on a Christmas tree. On our first date – in a moment of weakness and blind fascination– I told her about my dream.

"What date did you say you first had the dream?

"September 20, 1912.

"That's just about the time he was in Minneapolis."

"Who?"

"'Abdu'l-Bahá."

"Who?"

"The son of Bahá'u'lláh."

"Oh, that explains it."

"Sorry," she said, laughing. "Bahá'u'lláh was the founder of the Bahá'í Faith."

(*Animated.*) Needless to say, I was not interested. I was "up to here" with religion. And I certainly had no interest in something so oriental sounding as all that. I had only mentioned the dream because I wanted her to know all about me before I asked her to marry me. But she showed me a book that night. On September 20, 1912, the date of my first dream, this Persian gentleman, 'Abdu'l-Bahá, had spoken in Minneapolis, Minnesota only a short distance away from the little town in which I had lived and dreamed. He warned mankind to investigate the truth for themselves, and not to follow in the footsteps of those who accepted all things blindly. Later that same day, He had spoken in St. Paul, just across the river. He called upon mankind to be like the "fisherman Peter" and to fish energetically for the souls of men. Just as the man said in my dream: Be like Peter!

He takes out a picture from his things.

BILL: And <u>this</u> is a picture of 'Abdu'l-Bahá that Marguerite shared with me. This is the shiny man from my dream. Apparently, I had seen him at the train station that very day when we went to pick up my aunt. He made quite an impression on me. Evidently, he wasn't the Messiah, but he had come to the West to spread a message: not that Christ was coming, but that He had come... and gone!

He folds his arms and leans back or calls attention to an audience member who does.

BILL: That's exactly how I felt. No way. I've studied the Bible and I know what's supposed to happen. What, did the whole thing just come like a thief... in the night the way it says it will in Second Peter. Or, or, or in Revelations: Be watchful, or I will come as a thief. But then those are only a couple of references. There are hundreds of others. One Christian gentleman counted and between Old and New Testaments, he found 1843 references to the Second Coming. So what about the other 1841?

He picks up the magazine.

BILL: The woman is clever. Remember this: the magazine Marguerite left for me with the greatest headlines. She pinned a note inside: Don't read too late. By the way, did you know the Bahá'í Faith began in 1844? (*Beat.*) So next to the magazine she had placed this book: "The Bahá'í Proofs."

He opens the cover of the book and reads aloud.

BILL: "Let him who hath an eye to see, see; and him who hath an ear to hear, hear."

He closes the book quickly.

BILL: You see? The woman has pulled out all the stops. She's put the bounce on me, got me in this massive headlock, face to the canvas. Spiritually speaking, of course. The whole thing is very cordial and she's very sweet about it, but she knows that truth and time are on her side, and I'm left with something else: I dunno, denial and this sort of flailing about in this materialistic quagmire.

God called out to Abraham: Abraham! Abraham! And Abraham replied, "Here am I, my Lord." God called out to Jacob: Jacob! Jacob! And Jacob replied, "Here am I, my Lord." God called out to Bill Sears: Bill Sears! Bill Sears! And Bill Sears went *pkyooo*—

He makes a cartoonish exit. Hidden, he speaks aloud with the "God" voice.

BILL: "Bill Sears? What are you doing behind that door? Do you think I can't see you?" And Bill Sears replied: I'm comfortable!! Life's just started looking up for me. Finally, finally, I can pay my bills, I can support my family, and you want me to give all that up. I thought this success was the sign of your good-pleasure, your recognition of my work, the value of what I do. Why didn't you come when I wanted you? When I was calling out to you... from my rooftop? I don't want you now. My life's too complicated. (*A beat.*) As usual, silence.

My thoughts were another thing. I was finding it impossible to sleep. So I opened the book and read. And I read more. And I started to do some research. I keep it all here, away from Marguerite.

He takes out a box full of folders full of unorganized papers.

BILL: Don't tell her. She already suspects that I've swallowed hook, line and sinker. But this is only a little research. I think it would make a good book though... a mystery. I'll call it "The Case of the Missing Millenium."

Here, let me show you. (*He pulls out some papers from the box.*) These are some diagrams I made related to the prophecies, all pointing right smack to 1844. They say that this return is not of Christ's physical body descending from the sky, but that it's the same heavenly Spirit in a new body, just as human, and His new name is Bahá'u'lláh. Likewise, the sun and moon weren't literally going to lose their light. It was the light of Christ's spirit and teachings that was like a light to the world of the soul that would become darkened by superstition so that the truth couldn't be found. Corrupt religious leaders like fallen stars were no longer guiding lights to spiritual seekers. And so on.

As for Bahá'u'lláh, His life was an ocean of suffering, exile and imprisonment, but His words echo across these waters calling mankind together.

"The tabernacle of unity is raised. Regard ye not one another as strangers.

"Ye are the fruits of one tree, and the leaves of one branch."

"Lo, the Father is come, and that which ye were promised in the Kingdom is fulfilled."

When I hear His words, it's like I'm hearing the echo of the Prophets of old in their reply, "Here am I," but it's different, as if some great Reversal had taken place, where "Here am I, my Lord" has become "Here am I, *your* Lord."

So all of this, all of this, but what to do with it? I mean, if I believe this—This is big!—I should do something about it. I almost wish I could go back a hundred years and comfort those folks out on their rooftops. You're right! Today is the Day! It's just He's not coming the way you thought He would.

I've heard some talk that there's a call coming. A campaign to take this Message to all the countries and peoples of the world. To share the message with those who will hear it. And a little bubble rose up in both Marguerite and me, from the ocean floor in both of us rising higher and higher til it reached the top and gave up the ghost in a whisper that we both heard as "Africa."

But you know what? I'm sharing the message here. I'm in a unique position actually. People know me on the street. I come into hundreds of thousands of people's homes every week, and for a half an hour I can teach good moral and even spiritual lessons. And that guy in there, who writes the checks—he wants to pay me $50,000.00 a year to do it! Sounds perfect. I mean, come on! If there was ever a medium to spread a message, or a headline, or the greatest, most electrifying headline known to mankind, Television is the one. Right?

He has an idea that begins to animate his movement.

BILL: Okay, let's imagine what that might look like. It's next Sunday at 12 noon. We're ready to go. All quiet on the set! Going in 5, 4, 3—CBS Television presents "In the Park with Bill Sears" brought to you by Stewart Warner Televisions. Stewart Warner—your theatre of the world.

He pushes a couple of things aside, and makes a motion like the camera sweeping along the studio floor.

BILL: Hello, Albert!

(*Albert's voice*:) "Why do you look so happy, Bill?"

(*As himself*:) "Well, it's because the Lord of the Age has come." A deep silence fills the studio, and all eyes are on me. "That's right, boys and girls, Moms and Dads, Grams and Gramps all across America: Jesus has returned! Isn't that great news?" By now, the director has swallowed his wristwatch.

Paul, the puppeteer, has to make something up: "Who is Jesus?"

(*As himself*:) "Good question—you remember how a few years ago corporations like our sponsors changed the name of the holiday on December 25th, which is of course the most important consumer event of the year, to X-mas. Jesus is the one they X'd out." So the phone rings. It's some ad executive howling so loud I can hear him as I draw these diagrams about all the amazing prophecies, and then... (*Makes the sound of a sustained TV tone*) "Technical difficulties..." And I'm whisked away like Blanche Dubois in "Streetcar Named Desire": "I've always depended on the kindness of...sponsors!"

Here I am—got this message—the world is right there; no conceivable way to communicate it. What am I supposed to do? I feel like William Miller. Just give me a sign! (*Pause.*) Silence. As usual. You wouldn't make much of a radio man!

He picks up the "contract" letter.

BILL: The other day, after my *friend* talked to his boss... okay, I guess the jig is up. It's me. It was a flimsy device to begin with. So after the Boss basically said, no, you can't go and what about the 56 families and our contract with Stewart Warner Televisions? Marguerite has this idea that what we need is a prayer vigil. So for 19 days, we and our boys were supposed to pray hard. And if by the end of nineteen days, nothing happened, we'd resign ourselves to staying. So the clock is ticking. Today is Day 17. And still no sign on the horizon.

But you know what? One thing I've been learning in this "research" is that we're really not meant to dwell so much on signs or miracles. We're not here to accumulate miracles but virtues... like wisdom. That means learning by doing. Cause and effect. We make choices and we learn. Maybe it's as simple as this: This is not my dream. This is an inheritance that I have fulfilled and now... This isn't my dream at all. This isn't my dream at all.

Thank You for Your silence. If You spoke any louder, we'd all be struck dumb.

He picks up the beer bottle and moves to the sink.

BILL: Bless you, my dear old man.

He kisses the bottle, then pours down the drain. After a moment, he opens the letter.

BILL: What do you think? 45 or 50,000?

He reads.

BILL: Hm. "Dear Bill, Due to the fallout from their ongoing strike, Stewart Warner is canceling their sponsorship of *In the Park*." (*Trying to comprehend.*) Hoooohhh. Canceling? Canceling? How dare they cancel! Our ratings are great! Boy, I'm going to give them an earful.

He goes for the phone.

BILL: Ed Sullivan loved our show! You don't cancel a show that Ed Sullivan loves! (*Changing his demeanor.*) Hello, Mildred. Can you get me Stewart Warner? No, it's not a person, it's a company. I have no clue what their number is. City? No, sorry. How hard can they be to find? They sponsor my show. Who am I? Ed Sullivan! And your name was Winifred? Mildred, of course...

Look, this is not Ed Sullivan. Just say I'm Marco Polo and have a nice day.

He picks up the letter to re-read it.

BILL: "Bill, you had come to me asking about resigning. What I said still stands: It would be a tragedy to see you leave. But if you were looking for a green light to go, this would seem to be it."

He thinks.

BILL: On the rooftop, we scream 'break.' And when it breaks, when it really breaks, we cry and run inside. (*Throwing up his arms*) Aaaaah!

He runs offstage, and we hear him tearing around looking for something. He reenters with a slip of paper and goes to the phone. He picks it up and dials.

BILL: Hello, Mildred? This is Bill Sears at WCAU. Yes, in fact, there was a mad man up here—a lunatic howling from the rafters! Mildred, can you get me Long Distance, Minnesota, 3-5087? Thank you. (Pause.) Hello? Hello, Grandfather! This is Bill. (*To audience.*) He's still alive, in his nineties. (*To phone.*) Grandfather, I'm calling from the studio. I want to ask you if you would be a guest on my show this week. No, we could have a phone interview. All my listeners feel like they know you already. I've been telling them stories about you for years. (*He laughs.*) No, nothing good. How's Wednesday seven o'clock your time? I'll call you, okay? Because I want them to hear your voice before … Before I say goodbye. I'm saying goodbye to WCAU. I just decided. Marguerite and I have this wild idea of picking up and heading off. Africa, I think. Yes! (*He laughs excitedly.*) Why? Because… Because, well, in a nut shell: Christ has returned. His new name is Bahá'u'lláh. I am a Bahá'í, and I'm giving up everything to tell the world about His message. (*He listens.*) Grandfather? Grandfather? Oh. Did you fall? Oh. Good. (*To audience.*) Too much chin music on my pitch. I nearly knocked him over. (*Into phone.*) Nevermind, Grandfather. I'm going to send you something. A book. And we'll talk after you've read it. The thing is: I've finally found the answer to my dream… to our dream. I'll talk to you Wednesday. Okay? Bye bye.

I remember my father's face peering at me under the bedclothes on that night when he caught me reading the Bible under the covers. "Some day," I told him, "I'm going to find out all about God—something nobody knows. Then I'm going all over the world and tell people about my discovery."

He has packed up his things and goes to leave.

BILL: Here we go.

He turns off the light and exits.

ALTERNATE ENDING

[*The following may replace "Here we go" if the performer is so inclined:*

BILL: Thank you. You may think you haven't done much, but just your listening has been encouraging. And in your laughter, I hear the echo of divine happiness and I'm certain that God loves laughter. And we laugh until we cry – "three laughs and a tear" that's my motto – our heart overflowing with gratitude and we climb to the highest spot we can find and we throw wide our arms and we embrace the divine mystery and when we hear His call, we say finally, and with no hesitation, "Here am I, my Lord! Here am I!"

He laughs, turns off the light and exits.]

End of Play

Mr. William Sears on the set of "In the Park" (CBS)

Glossary

'Abdu'l-Bahá: eldest son of Bahá'u'lláh (1844–1921), the exemplar of the Bahá'í teachings, and the leader of the Faith from 1892 to 1921. (ab-DOL-ba-HA)

Alláh-u-abhá: Arabic for "God is most glorious," it is commonly used as a greeting used among Bahá'ís. (al-LAH-o-ab-HA)

Alláh-u-akbar: Arabic for "God is most great," it is a common phrase used in the Islamic world. It is part of the call to prayer and a common chant in moments of zeal. (al-LAH-o-AK-bar)

Auxiliary Board Member: An appointed position in the Bahá'í administrative order. With no clergy, the Bahá'í community organizes its affairs through elected consultative bodies (*see Spiritual Assemblies*) and those they appoint to serve particular community needs.

Áyatu'lláh: a title referring to the most powerful priests within Shí'ih Islam. (AH-ya-TO-la)

Báb, The: the Prophet-Herald of the Bahá'í Faith (1819-1850). His revolutionary teachings resulted in brutal suppression by the Persian government and clergy. He foretold the coming of Bahá'u'lláh and was ultimately executed by firing squad. (bahb**)**

Bábí: a follower of the Báb. (bah-BEE)

Bahá'í: a follower of the Bahá'í Faith, a religion that originated in Iran in the mid-19th Century. While Bahá'ís have faced periods of intense persecution in Iran, the Faith has spread widely around the world and is now practiced by many millions of people from all different backgrounds. (Buh-HIGH)

Bahá'u'lláh: the Prophet-Founder of the Bahá'í Faith and its most important figure (1817-1892). His given name was Mírzá Husayn 'Alí; Bahá'u'lláh is a title that means "The Glory of God." He was from a noble Persian family, but was banished in 1852 at the height of persecutions against Bábís. A prisoner and exile for forty years, Bahá'u'lláh wrote voluminously, providing guidance and laying the foundations for what is now a world-wide religious community. (ba-HA-o-LA)

Chádor: a dark, full-length body veil, almost like a tent, to be worn by Iranian women in public. It is intended to cover all but the face. (cha-DOOR)

Imám: "leader" in Arabic. (e-MAHM)

Iran: a country in southwest Asia, formerly known as Persia. (ir-RAHN)

Islamic call to prayer: One of the religious practices of Islam is for people to assemble several times a day to pray. The call to prayer is delivered by an individual, the *muezzin*, whose chanting signals the people to gather.

Kebáb: the Persian version of barbecue, with prepared meat skewered and cooked over an open flame. Traditionally, men make the kebáb. (ka-BOB)

Mosque: an Islamic house of worship. (mosk)

Mullá: a title for a religious leader of the *Shí'ih* branch of Islam. (mol-LA)

Naw-Rúz: the Persian New Year, a festival which begins on the first day of Spring. It's a time of joyfulness, generosity and hospitality. The Bahá'í calendar also features the first day of Spring as its Naw-Rúz. (no-ROOZ)

Persian: the predominant language of Iran. *Persia* is the old name for Iran, and the people are alternately called Iranians or Persians. (PER-zhin)

Qur'án (also **Koran**): the holy book of Islam. It is written in the Arabic language and consists of writings ascribed to the Prophet Muhammad, 570-632 C.E.. (kor-AHN)

Revolutionary Guard: a separate army raised up in Iran by the clergy during the Islamic Revolution of 1979. The Revolutionary Guard has been pivotal in establishing and maintaining the power of the clergy.

Riál: the official Iranian currency. In 1982, 1 Rial would be worth less than 5¢. (ree-AHL)

Ridván: An Arabic term for "Paradise," it is a 12-day festival beginning April 21 and is considered the holiest time of the Bahá'í calendar (RIZ-wahn)

Salaam: a greeting used in the Islamic world; Arabic for 'Peace.' (sa-LAHM)

Sháh: the King of Iran, often refers to Mohammad Reza Pahlavi (1919-1980)

Shí'ih (also **Shiah, Shiite**): that branch of Islam predominant in Iran and some of its surrounding regions. (SHE-uh)

Shíráz: a major city in the south of Iran, famous for its roses and its poets, especially Hafez and Sa'di. (She-RAHZ)

Spiritual Assembly: the consultative body of 9 individuals elected annually in local Bahá'í communities. Spiritual Assemblies are also elected on a national level. Assembly members became targets of persecution during the Islamic Revolution, and as result, Bahá'í administration has been suspended in Iran since the 1980s.

Túmán: a unit of Iranian money, worth 10 Ríál. In 1982, a bail payment of 200,000 Túmán would be worth from US$50,000 to $75,000. (TOO-mahn)

Yá Bahá u'l-abhá: Arabic for "O Glory of the Most Glorious," it is an invocation used by Bahá'ís in times of emergency, difficulty, elation, excitement, etc. (YA-ba-HA-ol-AB-ha)

Persian Pronunciation Guide

Observing just a few rules, a Persian accent can be fairly well approximated from a transliterated word or name. *

1. Vowel sounds

    a. When vowels have accents

      á   sounds like "a" in "father" or "o" in "dog"

      í   sounds like "ee" in "cheese"

      ú   sounds like "oo" in "shoot"

    b. When vowels have no accents

      a   sounds like "a" in "cat"

      e or i sounds like "e" in "get"

      o or u sounds like "o" in "go"

2. Consonant sounds

    a. Most consonant sounds are similar to English.

    b. Kh, Gh, and Q are guttural sounds, unfamiliar to English speakers. Appropriately, "kh" is midway between a "k" and an "h" and "gh" (and "q") is midway between a "g" and an "h." These are difficult sounds for many, so an easy compromise is pronouncing "kh" as "k," and "gh" (and "q") as "g."

3. Stress

    a. Give all syllables more or less equal stress.

    b. Fight the English tendency to speak in iambs or any other stressed / unstressed combination.

---

* For pronouncing character names, see the character list at the beginning of the play for proper transliteration. For Persian and Arabic terms without proper accents, see the Glossary.

Bibliography

'Abdu'l-Bahá, Paris Talks. London: UK Bahá'í Publishing Trust, 1972.

'Abdu'l-Bahá, Promulgation of Universal Peace. (Comp. by Howard MacNutt). Wilmette, IL: Bahá'í Publishing Trust, 1982.

'Abdu'l-Bahá, Selections from the Writings of 'Abdu'l-Bahá. (Trans. by Marzieh Gail and committee). Wilmette, IL: Bahá'í Publishing Trust, 1997.

'Abdu'l-Bahá, Some Answered Questions. (Trans. by Laura Clifford-Barney). Wilmette, IL: Bahá'í Publishing Trust, 1930.

A Dress for Mona (website). Ed. Mark Perry. Rev. Jan 2008. The Drama Circle. <http://www.adressformona.org>

Bahá'í National Youth Committee, Unrestrained as the Wind. Wilmette, IL: Bahá'í Publishing Trust, 1985.

Bahá'u'lláh, Epistle to the Son of the Wolf. (Trans. by Shoghi Effendi). Wilmette, IL: Bahá'í Publishing Trust, 1941.

Bahá'u'lláh, Gleanings from the Writings of Bahá'u'lláh. (Trans. by Shoghi Effendi). Wilmette, IL: Bahá'í Publishing Trust, 1952.

Bahá'u'lláh, The Kitáb-i-Aqdas (The Most Holy Book). Haifa: Bahá'í World Centre, 1992.

Bahá'u'lláh, The Kitáb-i-Íqán (The Book of Certitude). (Trans. by Shoghi Effendi). Wilmette, IL: Bahá'í Publishing Trust, 1931.

Bahá'u'lláh, The Seven Valleys and the Four Valleys. (Trans. by Marzieh Gail). Wilmette, IL: Bahá'í Publishing Trust, 1952.

Bahá'u'lláh, Tablets of Bahá'u'lláh, revealed after the Kitab-i-Aqdas. (Trans. by Habib Taherzadeh and committee). Wilmette, IL: Bahá'í Publishing Trust, 1988.

Bahá'u'lláh (et al), <u>Bahá'í Prayers</u>. Wilmette, IL: Bahá'í Publishing Trust, 1954.

Gulpaygani, Mirza Abu'l-Fadl, <u>The Bahá'í Proofs</u>. Wilmette, IL: Bahá'í Publishing Trust, 1983.

"IN THE PARK with Bill Sears." WCAU-TV (CBS), 1953? Dir. Joe Tinney, Jr. Perf. Bill Sears, Paul Ritts, Mary Ritts. Posted on Google Video by tvdays.com, Oct 2006. 29 minutes. <http://video.google.com/videoplay?docid=-6894375181616606671>

<u>Lights of Guidance: A Bahá'í Reference File.</u> (Ed. Helen Bassett Hornby). New Delhi: Bahá'í Publishing Trust, 1983.

Mahmudnizhad, Farkhundih, "Notes for a Film." (Trans. by Gloria Shahzadeh). Unpublished account of correspondence with Jack Lenz and Alexei Berteig, 2001.

National Spiritual Assembly of the Bahá'ís of Canada, <u>The Story of Mona: 1965-1983.</u> Thornhill: Bahá'í Canada Publications, 1985.

National Spiritual Assembly of the Bahá'ís of the United States, <u>Developing Distinctive Bahá'í Communities</u>. Evanston, IL: Office of Assembly Development, 2007.

Perry, Mark, <u>A Dress for Mona</u>. Shoreham, VT: 5th Epoch Press, 2002.

Roohizadegan, Olya, <u>Olya's Story</u>. Oxford: Oneworld Publications, 1993.

Sears, Marguerite Reimer, <u>BILL: A Biography of Hand of the Cause of God William Sears</u>. Eloy, AZ: Desert Rose Publishing, 2003.

Sears, Marguerite Reimer, <u>MARGUERITE… and more about BILL</u>. Eloy, AZ: Desert Rose Publishing, 2006.

Sears, William, <u>All Flags Flying</u>. NSA of the Bahá'ís of South Africa, 1985.

Sears, William, God Loves Laughter. Oxford: George Ronald, 1960.

Sears, William, Thief in the Night. Oxford: George Ronald, 1961.

The Bahá'í World, Vol. XIX: 1983-1986. Prepared under the supervision of The Universal House of Justice. Haifa: Bahá'í World Centre, 1994.

The Broadcast Pioneers of Philadelphia (website). <http://www.broadcastpioneers.com>

The Drama Circle (website). Ed. Mark Perry. Rev. Mar 2008. The Drama Circle. <http://www.dramacircle.org>

The Holy Bible, King James Version.

The Midnight Cry: William Miller & the End of the World. Dir. T.N. Mohan. Written by Ronald Alan Knott & Dennis O'Flaherty. VHS: Lathika International, 1994. DVD: Vision Video, 2006.

The Sixth Sense. Dir. M. Nnight Shyamalan. Written by M. Night Shyamalan. Perf. Bruce Willis, Haley Joel Osment. Buena Vista, 1999.

West Side Story. Dir. Robert Wise and Jerome Robbins. Music by Leonard Bernstein, lyrics by Stephen Sondheim. United Artists, 1961.

Zarandi, Nabíl ('Azam), The Dawn-Breakers: Nabil's Narrative of the Early Days of the Bahá'í Revelation. (Trans. and ed. by Shoghi Effendi). Wilmette, IL: Bahá'í Publishing Trust, 1932.

Mark Perry currently teaches playwriting and play analysis at the University of North Carolina at Chapel Hill, and he is a graduate of the University of Iowa's Playwrights Workshop. In 2002, he founded The Drama Circle, an organization focused on promoting Bahá'í-inspired theatre initiatives. His play *A Dress for Mona*, about the wrongful execution of a young Iranian woman, has previously been published in book and DVD forms, and both *A Dress for Mona* and his one-man show, *On the Rooftop with Bill Sears*, have toured throughout the United States and Canada. The revised *A New Dress for Mona* has since been produced in Finland, South Africa, and the United States. Mark received a 2005-06 North Carolina Arts Council Literature Fellowship for playwriting.